HUMAN NATURE and the FREEDOM of PUBLIC RELIGIOUS EXPRESSION
Stephen G. Post

Drawing on current research in science and religion, distinguished bioethicist Stephen G. Post provocatively argues that human beings are, by nature, inclined toward a presence in the universe that is higher than their own. In consequence, the institutions of everyday life, such as schools, the workplace, and the public square, are not justified in censoring the spiritual and religious expression that freely arises from the wellspring of the human spirit.

Post believes that the privatization of religious expression, coupled with the imposition of a secular monism, is a departure from true liberal democracy in which citizens are free to assert themselves in ways that manifest their full nature. Utilizing research in the neurosciences, psychiatry, the social sciences, and evolutionary psychology, he provides scientific information supporting the idea, familiar to theories of natural law, that religious expression and freedom are essential human goods. In developing this perspective, Post also engages in a critical conversation with secular existentialism.

Human Nature and the Freedom of Public Religious Expression offers an alternative to the views of political philosophers such as Richard Rorty, and educators such as John Dewey, who fail to acknowledge the unique contribution that religious language, when thoughtfully implemented, makes to the tone and content of public debate and education.

Human Nature

and the Freedom of
Public Religious Expression

Human Nature

and
the Freedom of
Public Religious
Expression

STEPHEN G. POST

UNIVERSITY OF NOTRE DAME PRESS
Notre Dame, Indiana

Manufactured in the United States of America

Library of Congress Cataloging-in-Publication Data
Post, Stephen Garrard, 1951–
Human nature and the freedom of public religious expression /
Stephen G. Post.
p.   cm.
Includes bibliographical references and index.
ISBN 0-268-03062-6 (pbk. : alk. paper)
1. Religion and science.   I. Title.
BL240.3 .P67   2003
323.44'2—dc21
2003004350

∞ *This book is printed on acid-free paper.*

Contents

Acknowledgments

I wish to thank Kevin J. Hasson, President of the Becket Fund for Religious Liberty, and Jonathan Rowland, Director of the Becket Institute at St. Hugh's College, Oxford University, for inviting me to write this essay while I was serving as a Senior Research Fellow at the Institute in the summers of 1998 and 1999. While at the Becket Institute, I appreciated the opportunity to converse with my colleague Raphaela Schmid, a philosopher of emerging significance in the Oxford community.

I wish to thank the John Templeton Foundation for providing a grant that supported me while at the Becket Institute. In particular, Charles L. Harper, Jr., D. Phil., Executive Director of the John Templeton Foundation, was instrumental in encouraging this exploration of themes at the interface of religion, human nature, and society.

I also wish to thank Robert J. Leisey of Detroit for early editorial comments and Barbara Juknialis of Cleveland for her very helpful copy editing. Special appreciation goes to Jeffrey L. Gainey of the University of Notre Dame Press, who made many useful suggestions as this essay evolved over several years.

Appreciation is also due to the Institute for Research on Unlimited Love, which supports the scientific study of compassionate love and service, and which provided me with the time to complete the final revisions of this work.

INTRODUCTION

Human Nature
and Public
Religious Expression

The integrated themes of this essay are twofold: *First, human nature appears to include a powerful spiritual and religious inclination; and second, a good society must include a correlative freedom for the individual to express this inclination in public domains, constrained only by laws against harming others.* These themes are perennial rather than novel, but so fundamental that it is wise to update them regularly, especially in a time when their truth is questioned.

As for the *first* theme, spiritual and religious consciousness is extremely strong at the dawn of the twenty-first century, despite the emergence of secular existentialism and the challenge of centuries of potent argument for atheism. It is so strong that we might just as well ask if the sun could more easily be plucked from the sky than the human sense of a creative higher presence be much diminished. Our human sense of a "Creative Presence" seems as vibrant as ever. Observation of contemporary and historical human experience makes plausible the hypothesis that human nature has evolved in such a remarkable way as to be turned toward a presence in the universe that is higher than its own. While we may never completely demonstrate the existence of such a Creative Presence through either scientific studies or philosophical argument, from the dawn of recorded history to the present the human perception and worship of such has not abated.

This persistent turning of human nature is now the subject of various explanatory models. Pascal Boyer, for example, advances an argument for the permanence of a religious inclination that is grounded in sociology and evolutionary psychology. His *Religion Explained* challenges the positivist's assumption that belief in a Creative Presence could be set aside in the human future.[1] Andrew Newberg, Eugene d'Aquili, and Vince Rause describe the ways in which the human brain appears "hard-wired" for spiritual and religious experiences in their work entitled *Why God Won't Go Away: Brain Science and the Biology of Belief.*[2] David Sloan Wilson, in *Darwin's Cathedral: Evolution, Religion, and the Nature of Society,* argues from the evolutionary biological perspective of group selection that a human society is like a competitive organism in which religion is a biologically, and culturally, evolved adaptation that enables the society to function as a *communitas* or internally altruistic unit—an adaptation that includes the element of out-group hostility, making exhortations to universal love of all humanity without exception both necessary and challenging.[3] Harold Koenig and colleagues, in their comprehensive *Handbook of Religion and Health,* rigorously critique the methodology of 1,200 separate scientific studies on the relationship between religion and health, rank them according to their reliability, and conclude that a sufficient number of very high-quality studies allow for the generalization that spirituality and religion contribute to psychological and physical flourishing.[4] While views of human nature vary, especially with regard to what is essential or inessential to it, these scientific works demonstrate that for various reasons religion is very deeply engrained in human nature.

This growing scientific appreciation for the permanence of spirituality and religion in *Homo sapiens* does not imply that the alternative secular image of the human is entirely implausible, nor that it lacks thoughtful defenders and deserves respect. Within the wide spectrum of perspectives on human nature, however, no one can seriously deny that a human inclination toward a Creative Presence is widely manifest and that the arguments made to encourage us to act contrary to this tendency have been relatively ineffective in the real world. The inclination appears too deep in human nature to be widely impeded by those who would wish to impede it, whether by philosophical argument or by the power of any government or judiciary that would futilely propose freedom from religion rather than freedom of religion.

Spirituality and religion are as significant as ever in human history, or more so, and take increasingly diverse forms. They appear inextinguishable. It can only be hoped that their beneficent manifestations will come to exclude all maleficent ones—a hope that pertains to *all* other forms of human expression. The great majority of human beings—although not all—seem to want communion with the Creative Presence, however variously interpreted and symbolized, and their own creativity and sense of purpose are often dependent on this communion. On balance, I do view the spiritual and religious inclination not only as essential to human nature but as generally beneficial and good.

Beneficial and good? Those who wish to censor public religious expression may make the common observation that religion is sometimes perverted through frenzied appeal to malicious human emotions, including hatred, arrogance, and insular loyalty. While the major world religions teach hospitality to the stranger and love for all humanity without exception, and while they characterize ultimate reality in terms of unlimited love, they do not easily live up to these moral ideals and metaphysical

assumptions. Wars between religions have never entirely sub-
sided, and we currently live in a time of global religious conflict.
We must all share in a healthy ambivalence about religiosity,
lauding it at its saintly best and condemning it at its violent worst.
But the solution to the recurring problem of religion's ability to
tap into violent emotions and out-group hatreds is not to be
found in the erroneous assumption that this inclination can
somehow be set aside as inessential, like casting off clothing. The
only answer rests in challenging people of all faiths within the
context of their particular sacred narratives to abide by the spiritual ideal of love for all humanity without exception—that is,
"unlimited" love. The spiritual and religious inclination is fundamentally enhancing of psychological well-being and moral idealism when it is not held hostage by group loyalties that demonize
outsiders or by the malicious and arrogant view that those who
conceptualize God in ways that differ from one's own tradition
should not be equally respected.

As for the *second* theme, the institutions of everyday life, including schools and universities, health care settings, the workplace, and the public square, are not justified in censoring the
spiritual and religious expression that freely arises from the wellspring of the human spirit. While free and open cultural, ethnic,
artistic, and literary expression are ubiquitous across the public settings of our lives—and inevitably in ways that someone
somewhere finds offensive—spiritual and religious expression
are often censored to please the intolerant fraction of a small
secular minority. But there is little said or symbolized in the
public world that does not annoy someone, and it is precisely
the tolerance of inevitable annoyances in all of our lives that distinguishes an open liberal democracy from closed authoritarianism. Those ardent secularists who would strip the public world of all reference to God as well as deny the freedom of
religious expression to others fail to appreciate the core aspect
of liberalism that they supposedly espouse. The proper demo-

cratic solution is for them to respectfully direct their attention elsewhere, rather than to engage in "religiophobia."

Public institutions and settings should be understood as an opportunity for human nature to find expression in its salutary dimensions. While "we the people"—a phrase sometimes used by John Courtney Murray, S.J.[5]—do not wish to see the establishment of any religion, neither do we wish for a culture and public world that is unfriendly to religion—for example, through removal of references to God in the seal of the state of Ohio, the Pledge of Allegiance, or the Declaration of Independence. We wish to live in a public world where ideas of God and of one nation under God are permanently ensconced in what has been called "ceremonial deism" by some courts. Here are found acceptable references to a nation's culturally religious tradition in a manner that does not violate the separation of church and state. In addition, "we the people" want to be able to respectfully integrate religious and spiritual commitments into free expression in public domains, including schools. "We the people" want a public world in which God is acknowledged, no religion is established, and freedom of religious expression is uncensored with the exception of actions contrary to the principle of nonmaleficence. Moreover, we should be grateful for this splendid American experiment, which has served the republic so well for so long.

This introduction provides an opportunity for a preliminary clarification of these two related themes and, secondarily, for comments on the nature of an essay in the tradition of the public intellectual.

Theme 1: A Religious Inclination as Epistemologically "Plausible"

As already stated, the idea that human beings are inclined toward a Creative Presence in the universe that is greater than their own—this is classically the idea of *Homo religiosus*—does not have to rest on a set of absolutely incontrovertible scientific facts about human nature but rather emerges from the weight of human experience and history. Epistemological appeal to experience, attentive to both the historical and the contemporary features of human expression and culture, is reasonably persuasive of an ineradicable spirituality often ensconced in the ritual, belief, and practice of formalized religion. Were spirituality and religion to disappear from the world, as Comte, Freud, Marx, and others long ago predicted, the appeal to human experience and history would result in a different conclusion about human nature. But their positivist predictions have never become reality. Epistemological rootedness in human experience is essential to the Aristotelian tradition and, in this context, demands recognition of the perennial prevalence of religious expression in the narrative of human history.[6]

The fact of religious inclination would be vivid to the impartial observer looking at the inhabitants of the planet for the first time. Rationalism separate from this observation strikes me as an unenviable project. We cannot ignore the larger spiritual tone of humanity and still claim to be grounded in observed human reality. Such observation is commonplace and offers nothing new. Yet *commonplace* is not used here with a negative or pejorative meaning. Instead, I wish to bolster the commonplace, to move such observations into the category of the fundamentally true and even sublime.

This spiritual tone was observed a century ago by the British biologist Julian Huxley, who, while an agnostic, nevertheless acknowledged that the human capacity to construct religions is remarkable, persistent, and even inspiring. Thus Huxley wrote that "since natural selection is the sole or main method of biological evolution, and since it can only operate to produce results of biological utility, it is clear that the mental properties of organisms are not mere useless by-products, but must be of value to their possessors."[7] Among these human capacities religion can be included as a useful aspect of evolution: "These include the capacity to construct religions in the broad sense — systems of attitude, in which knowledge can be combined with ideals and imaginatively fused with our deep spiritual emotions to form a stable network of sentiments and beliefs, which in turn influence behavior and help to determine moral and practical action."[8] Huxley was intrigued rather than offended at the human capacity to create what he called "noetic integrators" to give orientation and direction to life.

That human nature turns toward a Creative Presence is further evidenced by the fact that so much developed human reflection focuses on the existence of such a presence. If human nature were different, if we were not inclined to ask questions of ultimate meaning and ultimate reality in a context that took this Creative Presence into consideration, then the annals of human philosophical and theological thought would be filled with very different subject matter than they are. In this sense, the fact that we trouble to think so often and so deeply about the God question hints that on some existential level we intuit such a divine presence. Many people see about them the overwhelming beauty of the earth and of the universe, which inclines them to suppose that artistry involves a Creative Presence. St. Paul wrote that "ever since the creation of the world his eternal power and divine nature, invisible though they are, have been understood and seen through the things he has made" (Rom. 1:20). We appear inclined to speculate ontologically, metaphysically, and theologically, and this is what one would expect from a creature with an innate worshipful tendency. In moments of severe illness, for example, we seem widely inclined to ask questions like "How can a good God allow bad things to happen to good people?" The pervasiveness of such speculation across cultures and times hints at an essential human tendency rather than a purely cultural artifact, although culture is surely influential.

We do see periods in which certain intellectual circles set these sorts of speculations aside. But as Huston Smith argues, questions about ultimate reality and ultimate meaning are grounded in humanness and resist abolition:

> Wherever people live, whenever they live, they find themselves faced with three inescapable problems: how to win food and shelter from their natural environment (the problem nature poses), how to get along with one another (the social problem), and how to relate themselves to the total scheme of things (the religious problem). If this third issue seems less important than the other two, we should remind ourselves that religious artifacts are the oldest that archeologists have discovered.[9]

Smith writes that religious worldviews include the sense that "human beings are *the less who have derived from the more*,"[10] which means that they are not perceiving themselves as "*the more that has derived from the less*."[11] In our modern world, continues Smith, science has presumed to answer by denial all metaphysical or "Big Picture" spiritual questions.[12] It has created an antimetaphysical world in which even the philosophers "tend to assume that scientists are in a better position to see the whole of things than they themselves are."[13] Smith describes a modern "tunnel" vision that attempts to exclude "Big Picture" thinking: the floor is scientism, the left wall is higher education, the roof is the media, and the right wall is the law. But the human rational inclination to raise metaphysical questions cannot be suppressed, argues Smith, and it now increasingly explodes through the tunnel walls. Indeed, considerable numbers of scientists are themselves now asking metaphysical questions.

While appeal to human experience suffices as a ground-work for asserting a spiritual and religious inclination, on an important secondary level, science may be fairly marshaled to further substantiate this assertion. As one of the most cautious judges of cosmological and evolutionary science, Robert Wright, states, "Is there some grand goal that life on earth was 'designed' to realize? I think the reasons for answering yes are stronger than many people—especially many scientists and social scientists—realize. Still, as I've already suggested, the question is slippery, and answers to it must be speculative."[14] Science can study human nature in all its aspects from culture to neuroscience, and it can examine cosmology and other areas of physics to see if there is any hint of a Creative Presence, as Einstein thought there was in his oft-quoted statement "God does not play dice with the universe."

Leading scientists do sometimes offer spiritual speculation on the facts they uncover. Physicist Paul Davies is among those many physicists for whom the constants of the universe raise questions about "the origin and meaning of the universe, the place of human beings in the world, and the structure and or-ganization of nature"—questions that require "rational and dis-passionate analysis."[15] A leading physicist conversant with the relevant data, Davies, who reports never having had a mystical experience, concludes that the "existence of mind in some or-ganism, on some planet in the universe is surely a fact of fun-damental significance. Through conscious beings the universe has generated self-awareness. This can be no trivial detail, no minor by-product of mindless, purposeless forces. We are truly meant to be here."[16] In another text he puts the point a little differently after an extensive analysis of the origins of life, sug-gesting "a self-organizing and self-complexifying universe, gov-erned by ingenious laws that encourage matter to evolve towards life and consciousness. A universe in which the emergence of thinking beings is a fundamental and integral part of the overall scheme of things. A universe in which we are not alone."[17] What is Davies's fundamental observation? He points to the long list of "indispensible prerequisites" for the existence of our species, including chemistry, temperature, energy, ozone, location in the cosmos, electromagnetic forces, and the like, all fine-tuned like some great symphony from which a creature with our capacities would eventually emerge: "We could regard our existence as an accident of almost unbelievable improbability— for out of all possible worlds, our universe happens to choose just that highly ordered arrangements of matter and energy that keeps the cosmos cool enough for life."[18] Why are the laws of nature what they are, so as to generate life? Increasingly, scientists are drawn by their research to ask metaphysical questions that can no longer be the exclusive domain of theologians and philosophers.[19]

History, experience, and the very readiness to raise metaphysical questions at least point in the direction of a Creative Presence. If human nature really is turned toward God like a flower toward the sun, one can intelligently surmise that this inclination arose evolutionarily in response to some objective and attracting feature of the universe. While this is indeed a highly speculative transposition, moving us quickly into the area of metaphysical speculation on the nature of a God and ultimate reality, it is not scientifically odd to think that complex inclinations do not evolve without some real and objective point of reference in the wider environment. Of course I suggest no formal proof, compelling evidence, or linear argument to support this idea. I only wish, in humility, to indicate its plausibility.

Two analogies may be useful here. The God tendency would be like the turning of a sunflower. As the sun rises, the sunflower turns to the east, and as the sun journeys west across the sky the flower follows it. The sunflower has evolved this way because it gets a flow of benefit from being sun-pointed. So the spiritual instinct turns us toward the Creative Presence. This instinct would also be like the wick of a lamp. It can burn dimly or brightly according to whether the wick is turned down or up, and in some the flame can be extinguished. Yet the wick remains. Thus St. Augustine wrote, "Man is one of your creatures, Lord, and his instinct is to praise you."[20] However forgetful we are of the Creative Presence, the instinct remains and memory can be rekindled. It is often rekindled in the context of group worship, replete with sacred symbols and rituals.[21]

In 1932 the anthropologist R. R. Marett first suggested that *Homo sapiens* would better be designated *Homo religiosus*.[22] Spiritual-religious concerns are present among the earliest evidences of human behavior, and we know of no human societies over the entire course of history that are devoid of such concerns. Spiritual and religious human expression dates back to at least 60,000 B.C.E.,[23] indicating that it can be respected for its staying power alone. Whatever continuities exist between human beings and other advanced species, we alone pray and worship.

Central to this essay is the classical natural law concept that spiritual-religious expression is the outgrowth of an essential human propensity that is far from irrational and that cannot be long inhibited without incidence of revolt or a generalized failure in individuals and society to most fully thrive. This is not to suggest that the person in whom the religious impulse is inhibited cannot live a good and moral life—in some instances a life more laudable than those religious counterparts who manifest harmful absolutisms and destructive intolerance. Nevertheless, without wishing to deny the above ambiguity, I would concur with the words of John Hick, for the human being is "a religious animal," and in its highest expression, this spirituality reorganizes the self's priorities and elevates it.[24]

Theme 2: A Correlative Freedom

This essay is about the freedom of religious expression in the light of a plausible hypothesis about human nature. In virtually all the domains of everyday life, religious as well as nonreligious people wish to be what and who they are in their particularity, consistent with the rules of respect and tolerance. While secularists remind us that in some parts of the world at some points in time they themselves have been censored, this does not justify silencing those citizens who are spiritual and religious. We must of course be cognizant of the extent to which any image of human nature, whether secular or sacred, can be and has been used as a tool of political oppression. This is the constant and necessary refrain of the deconstructionists. Yet the abuse of power by those who consider themselves the bearers of human normalcy is a matter best addressed by affirming and perfecting the preventive structures of pluralistic liberal constitutional democracy, rather than by imposing a secular monism.

Those who wish to censor religious expression from the public world must make every effort to acculturate the young to their vision of the future. If the young can be taught to accept the view that their speaking and behaving as though not religious is in no way a violation of their human nature and dignity, then censorship becomes permanently tolerable to them. This is why adamant secularists are so proactive in the public schools, where, contrary to all other public institutions, such as the halls of Congress, the Veterans Administration health system, and the military, there are neither chaplains nor sites for prayer and meditation.

The Public School Problematic as a Case in Point

While beliefs and practices (including prayer) pertaining to ultimate meaning should not be required of students, students should retain an absolute negative right—that is, a right to noninterference—to voluntarily engage in such activities. They should be free to say grace before meals; read from whatever scripture or secular source they hold dear; pray or meditate alone or in groups during free time; wear Stars of David, yarmulkes, crosses, or any other meaningful symbols both sacred and secular; and express religious or secular ideas in their homework assignments or artwork. Such expression can only elevate the currently diminished moral and ethical tone of some schools; it will certainly make school life and academics more interesting as students become aware of one another's intriguing beliefs about matters of ultimate meaning, whether sacred or secular. The idea that those students who do not share the religious faith of the expressive individual are somehow placed under hardship by possibly witnessing such expressions is as absurd as suggesting that when I say grace before my meals in restaurants I thereby trample on the rights of those at another table. Moreover, witnessing such free expressions might result in curiosity, conversation, and the sharing of ideas that would offer an alternative to the media-shaped cult of violence that gives rise to shootings such as the one at Columbine.

With regard to public institutions, many Americans have especially struggled with the censorship imposed in the public schools, and some have had to resort to school vouchers as a way of freeing their children from the grip of such radical censorship. It is encouraging that in one important case decided in 2001, *Good News Club v Milford Central School,* the United States Supreme Court properly ruled that if the Girl Scouts or the 4-H Club are permitted to meet on school property after classes, so also must a group of students who wish to pray or read Scripture be allowed to do so.[25] In a six-to-three decision, the Supreme Court extended to elementary schools the same principles it has applied to public colleges and high schools: religious expression is protected against discrimination by the First

Amendment, and it is therefore entitled to access on a neutral basis to all public facilities that are open to secular forms of expression. The Court concluded that allowing the Good News Club to use a room in a public school building on the same basis as other voluntary organizations ensures neutrality rather than threatening it. The Court rejected the baseless argument that equal access would be mistaken for official school endorsement of religion, since this sort of argument could be equally applied to absolutely any voluntary gathering. There is no constitutional crisis when a religious organization is afforded the same rights as other organizations, however much the Court's critics tried to claim one.[26] The Court was not calling for an establishment of religion; instead, it was calling for equal respect, equal access, and nondiscrimination against religious expression in institutional contexts where clearly the only thing that violates the establishment clause is the official establishment of a philosophy of secular humanism held by few but imposed on all.

A positive recognition of—as well as an affirming neutrality between—the religious and secular images of human nature is required in any liberal constitutional democracy, and it must begin in the schools. It seems, however, regrettable that in the last several American decades neutrality has been distorted into its contrary—the affirmation of secular expression at the expense of spiritual and religious expression. The result is an impoverished public domain that fails to reflect the richness and variety of the human condition and the full pluralism of liberal democracy.

The schools have been especially vulnerable to this diminution. They become an early seedbed for privatization: that is, our public institutions force religion in general and religion in its particularistic forms out of sight and out of mind. Thus many Americans know nothing or next to nothing about faiths different from their own and are denied a fuller understanding of the Muslim, Buddhist, or Sikh who stands next to them. It is perhaps only in a time of catastrophe, when a particular religion falls short of universal love and spirals downward into violence, that we seek to remediate our ignorance. If the model of all Veterans Administration hospitals, hospices, private schools, airports, and military bases was applied, it would be laudable for public schools to create interfaith centers replete with the symbols of all worldviews, whether major or minor, and to make chaplains available for students in need. Students could choose to spend free time in such a center. In private universities, including ones such as the Massachusetts Institute of Technology, which has no religious history, this sort of center is now becoming the norm.[27] Student-initiated postings of the Golden Rule in its religious and philosophical contexts, or of the Ten Commandments and other similar sets of spiritual and moral rules, should be welcomed as forms of public meaningful expression, although no single expression should be granted preferential status by the institution.

James W. Fraser, Director of the Center for Innovation in Urban Education at Northeastern University in Boston, points out the need for just such a new culture in the public schools:

> Too often school people, especially liberals and progressives, have responded to the issue of religion in the schools by hoping for absolute silence. Acting more like Victorian prudes in the face of reference to sex than true progressives, they have not embraced the potential of religious difference and discourse. Prior to the 1960s, many school leaders took the same approach to issues of race and sex. They seemed to say, "Maybe if we never mention the subject we will be okay." This continues to be the approach to religion in far too many schools at the end of the twentieth century. Yet this approach is not helpful. The child who is militantly secular or an atheist, or who is a Protestant fundamentalist,

or who is a Unitarian, a conservative Catholic, Muslim, Janist, Buddhist, Adventist, Presbyterian, or Jew, or any one of so very many other traditions; each must be welcomed not only as a person with an equal right to respect and a public education but as a citizen who has his or her own unique contribution to make to the school and to society, a contribution which every other child will be poorer if they fail to understand.[28]

It is oppressive to create a school environment in which children from secularist families are the only ones who feel comfortable and at home. We should celebrate those students with different religious beliefs, rather than coercively construct the thin and false environment of John Dewey's "common faith" of secularism. Fraser is critical of John Dewey's notion of this "common faith": "Dewey could not help seeing a more theistic world view not as a democratic right in need of respect, but as simply the stubborn reaction of fundamentalists in need of the ministrations of good progressive educators."[29] While there is a side to most of us concerned with religious conflicts in the world that utters the phrase "God save the world from fundamentalists," rigidity of belief does not justify censorship, and it is the very openness of a pluralistic institution to such voices that invites the fundamentalist to gradually explore other perspectives.

The diminution of freedom of religious expression in schools is deeply concerning. For example, as a reward for being a good reader, first-grader Zachary Hood was told he could read a story of his choice to his class. When he chose the story of Jacob and Esau, the teacher balked on the grounds that a religious story would violate the wall of separation between church and state. Zachary's parents brought a lawsuit against the teacher and the Medford, New Jersey, public school system. Zachary's defenders pointed out that the schools are misreading constitutional law. Similarly, a ninth-grade student in Dixon, Tennessee, wanted to write an essay about the life of Jesus in her English class. The teacher said the topic was unacceptable and flunked the girl when she refused to write on another topic. These cases are not about religious practices or witnessing; they are about religious children wanting to use the stories of their traditions in a fitting and interesting academic way.[30]

Secular hospitals provide referrals to clergy and expect physicians to be respectful of patient belief systems; the armed services provide pastoral care for those who desire it; yet in the public schools spirituality is driven underground. Why can't a public school allow students to express their religious beliefs in a civil, pluralistic, and respectful way? If public schools want to thrive and retain students, they need not make efforts to encourage religion; like other public institutions, however, they must make efforts to respond to students' beliefs. Otherwise, the students will feel invalidated and marginalized, as though their precious and life-guiding beliefs rested on pure error.

The public celebration of religious diversity in schools and elsewhere can only make life more engaging and informative for us all.[31] At city hall, the library, and schools, displays of manger scenes and menorahs should be a source of public delight, as should be proclamations of the Islamic Ramadan. In such a public world we would have the joy of expressing our deepest selves and of honoring this expression in others. This is a world in which we actually know one another's core values and ideals.

In my town of Shaker Heights, Ohio, the annual public tree lighting in Shaker Square features the costumed figures of Frosty the Snowman and Shamu the White Whale from Sea World of Ohio. Banished are all spiritually and ethically meaningful symbols and expressions, both religious and secular, that could collectively elevate the life of our community. We know nothing much about anyone, and the lighting event is both uninteresting and trivial. Such trivialization is not without consequences in a liberal democracy, for it hampers the deeper mutual understandings that contribute to civic peace. We should crowd onto the canvas of public life a spiritual catalogue of the family of humanity. This experience can help diminish any tendencies among some believers to disrespect and even harm people of other faiths and traditions.

Shaping an Essay

In reading a meditative essay or a social commentary, rather than a scholarly treatise that presents a thesis and then argues it according to generally accepted scholarly principles, one can expect that the author may integrate material from a variety of sources that are somewhat interconnected, pointing out relationships and suggestive areas for future analysis. To some degree, the sources selected will inevitably reflect the interests of the author but they should all contribute to thoughtfulness about the themes under consideration.

The first chapter of this essay develops some phenomenological and emerging scientific claims about human nature, spirituality, and religion in the context of illness. The religious inclination is highly evident in time of severe diagnosis or injury. While this initial point of focus may surprise the reader, the health care context is very heavily researched by social scientists interested in patient spirituality and religion. It is without question here that the best social scientific research studies are available on *Homo religiosus,* and the appeal to these data adds to my overall argument in a way that attention to schools or workplace will not achieve. In this analysis of the experience of illness, I do not wish to reduce spirituality and religion to fear and anxiety; rather, it is precisely in such circumstances that ordinary routines of daily life are pushed aside to reveal something about human nature—a turning toward a Creative Presence that is usually of lesser existential significance when we bury ourselves in the preoccupations of the routines. These routines are ultimately illusory. It is in "limit situations"—Karl Jaspers's term—that our loss of control over events strips us of illusions and that the spiritual and religious nature of the human being is most evident.

A second chapter takes up the scientifically rudimentary but nevertheless substantial neurological accounts of spiritual and religious experiences, which suggest that such experiences were "hard-wired" into the human brain as it emerged over the course of evolution. New data on the brain and religious experience only point out how deeply ensconced such experience is in human nature and show that it is grounded in evolved brain pathways. This fact does point toward certain metaphysical questions.

A third chapter draws on the prior two in updating the classical natural law theory of human nature, which includes the assertion of Thomas Aquinas that human beings are naturally inclined to God. The mere fact that every known human society in history, at one stage or another, includes religious origin myths and rituals, indicates that religion is a natural human phenomenon. But the emergent data discussed in the preceding chapters allow us to begin to place the inclination toward a Creative Presence on a little firmer scientific foundation. Aquinas himself drew on the life sciences of his time.[32] In other words, it will be argued that the idea of *Homo religiosus* is not just a matter of belief and speculation on the part of theologians but one that has serious groundings in common human experience and increasingly in empirical studies.

With this updated perspective on an innate human inclination as background, I next turn toward the importance of religious freedom. Catholic social thought has generally argued that religious freedom is justified by an appeal to human nature itself. This distinguishes Catholic thought from the evangelical view of religious freedom as necessary for religions to remain vibrant through selective competition, from the Jeffersonian liberal view that human beings have a negative right to be left alone on matters of conscience and meaning, from the general appeal to autonomy, and from the libertarian view that the state is always in need of restraint. Of course, I concur with all of these other views and appeal to them where fitting. But the theme put forth here is that freedom of religion, and of religious expression in public domains, is a necessary manifestation of a central feature of human nature itself. In chapter 4 I develop arguments for a liberal democratic future in which spiritual-religious expression is not censored but celebrated and allows us all to respectfully understand and appreciate one another in our fullness.

In discussing the public and political implications of *Homo religiosus,* I touch only lightly on the judiciary because this is not my focus, although it would be rewarding if the arguments about human nature developed in this work proved influential in the legal domain. Furthermore, because I am concerned with religious expression in the public world (e.g., in the context of politics, schools, academic debate, social work, the workplace, and hospitals), "church and state" (i.e., relations between institutions) is not a principal focus. This essay is concerned with two kinds of conviction (commitment) that meet in the person of the politician-believer, the student-believer, and the like.

My overall goals in this work are (1) to update the idea that human beings are naturally inclined toward a Creative Presence on experiential and scientific grounds insofar as evidence permits, and (2) to extrapolate the implications of this idea for the expression of religion in public domains. In the final analysis, I do not believe that the freedom of religious expression *requires* a scientific account of a natural religious propensity because respect for the autonomy of citizens to speak and live in public and in private as they so wish is *alone* a sufficient ethical principle upon which to ensure such freedom of expression. Yet the emergence of a scientific case for *Homo religiosus* does provide an additional argument in support of freedom of religious expression, or at least provides reasons to resist the trivialization of this freedom, for such spiritual expression now represents a highly demonstrated aspect of human nature rather than a mere subjective whim.

Most people want to express a sense of the miracle of existence that has become patent to so many physicists convinced that there is a place for a Creative Presence in cosmology.[33] People thirst on some level for harmony between their lives, values, purposes, and the source of all that is. They want to integrate the Cosmos and the Polis toward Cosmopolis in whatever religious belief system provides a venue, and when they find this integration they do not want it privatized. They want to tell about this discovery of the miracle of existence, do good deeds, and speak and express themselves freely in all spheres. Society and law should celebrate this diversity of venues.

CHAPTER ONE

The Religious Inclination in "Limit Situations"

How does one add formal research data to the loosely empirical observation that the human creature is inclined by its very essence toward a presence in the universe that is higher than itself and that the God-centered fulfillment of this inclination is contributory to individual well-being? I select the research context of religion and health as a scientific starting point because numerous studies of increasing sophistication have emerged and because it is here that one can more easily examine the religious inclination in its more intense manifestations against the background of severe diagnoses, injury, and dying. These are all "limit situations," a concept that is commonly used in modern theology to refer to circumstances of major disruption in which one's control over outcomes is severely diminished or entirely eradicated.

A 2002 poll touches on the significance of limit situations with regard to spirituality in the wake of September 11, 2001. In the poll, more than four of five Americans say that they have "experienced God's presence or a spiritual force" in their proximity; 46 percent indicate that this has happened to them many times.[1] Those polled represent a sampling of persons from almost every major culture, faith, and nationality. The poll also indicates *that the intensity and seriousness about spirituality and religion rose somewhat in the wake of the attack of September 11, 2001*—a "limit situation" in which the routines of life were dramatically interrupted by perilous and uncontrollable circumstances. This is not surprising because numerous social science studies show that spirituality and religion are especially pronounced and significant under such circumstances, in which people frequently turn to God, however defined, who does have things under control.[2]

The data on the place of spirituality and religion in human nature are best developed in studies on health and coping with severe illness. Immanuel Jakobovits, Chief Rabbi of the British Commonwealth of Nations, wrote in his classic *Jewish Medical Ethics* that "disease forges an especially close link between God and man; the Divine Presence Itself, as it were, 'rests on the head of the sickbed.'"[3] Why this observation? Is it merely the musing of a theist? Or is it objectively true?

As existentialist theologians point out, human beings wish to protect themselves through the security of daily routines that provide a perception of order and control over existence. Routines and ordinary life goals, both of which fulfill the need for security, quickly evaporate when serious illnesses break into life. We fragile human beings are subject to critical and life-threatening contingencies against which we are entirely powerless. Our protective routines deflect our anxiety over this incontrovertible fact of life. These routines, however, are illusory from the existential perspective. We gain insight into this illusory quality when the catastrophic breaks into our hitherto controlled patterns. It is at these critical life junctures that spirituality and religion become even more evident in the lives of remarkably large numbers of people, although their importance is readily apparent even in periods of secure routine.

Severe illness explodes our routinized lives into fragments, leaving us unprotected and painfully aware of the limited control we possess over the course of events in our own bodies and in the bodies of others. The cares and occupations of daily life can no longer be depended on to shield us through diversion. People then draw more heavily than usual on God, however symbolized, who is in the fullest sense still in control.

Much of this chapter draws on social scientific data on the ways in which illness gives rise to heightened spirituality and religious expression. These data are often derived from methodologically valid social scientific studies that have frequently been verified through duplication of findings.[4] I do not take up studies on the efficacy of prayer because of their methodological and conceptual limitations, as well as their complete irrelevance to my argument. The results of prayer studies can best be described as inconsistent and contradictory, which perhaps buttresses the theological argument that only the most irresponsible deity would indulge our various whimsical and often selfish petitions. Rabbinic opinion asserts that to assume that God must answer a prayer is presumptuous and represents an arrogant transgression. The Hebrew Bible and the Talmud indicate that prayer is thought to be efficacious if offered by the proper person at the proper time with the proper intent and under the proper circumstances. When David prayed for the recovery of his son, the boy died (2 Sam. 12:16). What is of relevance to my inquiry is not the outcome of the prayer, but the mere fact that David is inclined to pray for the sick and dying.

Fortunately, social science studies on the human inclination toward a Creative Presence in time of illness are more scientifically reputable, and their findings are fairly impressive. As patients deal with situations that challenge them and their self-definition—for example, major medical illness or death—questions of meaning often arise in the context of spiritual beliefs. Illness is a major event that disrupts careers, family life, and enjoyments, causing patients to question their purpose in life. Since spirituality, which is often expressed in religious symbols, beliefs, and practices, forms the basis for meaning and purpose in the lives of many patients, physicians observe that the physician "who would heal cannot choose whether to confront religious variables in practice; they are operating whether recognized or not."[5]

Dying, a natural outcome of many illnesses, amplifies these spiritual concerns, and for this reason hospice programs routinely include a major role for pastoral care. In the *ars moriendi*, or art of dying, restoration of wholeness is often enhanced by spirituality, leading ultimately to a peaceful death. The emergence of spirituality and religion in the illness context leads many to metaphysical speculations—for example, if there is a Creative Presence in the universe, then why is this illness striking down my loved one or myself? There will be those who in their dying revolt angrily against spirituality and religion in a flurry of resentment against God. Yet even in such cases it cannot be denied that the question "Oh God, how can you be letting this happen?" surfaces routinely and with remarkable power. The very fact that this anger suddenly emerges is itself an indication of an essential spiritual and religious nature, however much the person is caught up in the throes of denial, resentment, and dashed hopes for the future. (All human beings are frail and mortal, and in this sense "bad" but inevitable things like illness and death happen to all of us. The question "Why do bad things happen to good people?" is foolish because such things are inevitable and ubiquitous.)

In this chapter, I will review empirical data on spirituality and illness in the contexts of substance abuse, mental health, physical health, and dementia. I am less interested in how spiritual life affects illness outcome than I am in how illness seems to bring spirituality and religion to the surface as a means of coping. My discussion of the emergence of spirituality and religion in illness will necessarily suggest the importance of allowing the free expression of spirituality in clinical contexts—arguments that can be extended to other contexts as well. I will begin, however, with a more formal discussion of "limit situations."

Jaspers on Limit Situations

Karl Jaspers (1883–1969), a physician, psychologist, and philosopher, has described "certain decisive, essential situations, which are the unavoidable condition of finite human existence. . . . These situations, which at the limits of our existence are everywhere felt, experienced, conceived, we therefore call 'limit-situations.'"[6] What are these situations? In his *Philosophy,* published in 1932, Jaspers enumerates several limit situations and elaborates on the description given in *Psychologie der Weltanschauungen:*

> Situations such as: that I cannot live either without struggle or without suffering, that I ineluctably take guilt upon myself, that I must die—these I call limit situations. They do not change except in their appearance; as applied to our existence they possess finality. . . . They are like a wall against which we butt, against which we founder.[7]

Suffice it to say that limit situations are those undesired situations that are not of our making and from which we cannot escape.

Jaspers finds limit situations doubly important. First, they serve to illuminate *Existenz*—the aspect of my being that gives me absolute uniqueness and by virtue of which I am related to God. As Soren Holm has put it, "Existenz without relation to Transcendence (God) has no meaning."[8] Adolph Lichtigfeld, who was active in the rabbinate and an important Jaspers scholar, has expanded Holm's claim: "Principles of religion were disclosed to man in these ultimate [limit] situations, in which he found himself,"[9] as in the wilderness circumstances of the Jews. Second, the experience of limit situations brings us to an awareness of a Creative Presence through an awareness of ourselves as foundering and utterly dependent.

Suffering, especially suffering secondary to chronic, debilitating, and often life-threatening illness, is a limit situation, one that Jaspers endured from his early adolescence. Of himself, he has written: "Not only is the invalid more conscious of man's finiteness and his radical dependence, in his case it is something qualitatively different. Not even for a day can he depend on himself as existence."[10] The experience of complete dependence, first described by Friedrich Schleiermacher in the nineteenth century and manifested in the personal life and philosophy of Jaspers, leads to an acknowledgment of dependence on God insofar as one is aware of self as *Existenz.* In *Way to Wisdom,* Jasper puts it thus: "To ultimate [limit] situations we react either by obfuscation or, if we really begin to apprehend them, by despair and rebirth: we become ourselves by a change in our consciousness of being."[11] Thus, in limit situations, the consciousness of a presence beyond and above ourselves is essentially natural to human existence.

Without reducing spirituality and religion to the context of limit situations, Jaspers's point is that under such conditions the deeply evolved and permanently present impulses of spirituality and religion in the human being are set free to reach toward a Creative Presence.

Examples of Empirical Data in Limit Situations of Severe Illness

Research data presented here appear to substantiate the claim that an inherent human propensity is freed in limit situations of illness. Although other aspects of illness could also be included, I refer here to the limit situations of substance abuse, mental illness, physical illness, and death and dying. The studies referred to are considered to be methodologically sophisticated and verifiable.

Substance Abuse

From the perspective of the *Homo religiosus* thesis, substance abuse represents an imitation of religious experience that makes a mockery of the reality. It can be surmised that certain substances involve the same neurological correlates that are associated with genuine religious experience. Few circumstances in life are more limiting and catastrophic than a significant drug addiction, which destroys hopes, achievements, and relationships and which seems to allow no escape. In such a context, religion should be a major contributor to healing. As Dietrich Bonhoeffer often commented, human beings have within them a God-sized space that only God can fill, however much we attempt to fill this space with various substitutes.

An early empirical study of the power of religious experience and faith to overcome the addict's craving for heroin was funded in the late 1970s by the National Institute on Drug Abuse. In this study, directed by David P. Desmond of the University of Texas, heroin addicts undergoing standard treatment at a local hospital were divided into two groups, only one of which consisted of addicts who later joined inpatient religious recovery programs. One year into recovery, the subjects in the religious recovery programs were nearly eight times more likely to report abstinence from opiates than those subjects who received the purely secular treatment.[12]

Psychiatrist George E. Valliant of Harvard Medical School, another leading researcher, demonstrated the "enormously important therapeutic principle" of religiosity in recovery from alcoholism.[13] As fellow psychiatrist Harold G. Koenig underscores,

"Most psychiatrists recognize that the oldest and most successful recovery organization, and the model for all "Twelve Step" programs, Alcoholics Anonymous, depends heavily on God and divine grace to achieve and preserve sobriety."[14] Step 11, recited at each meeting, is a public affirmation that recovering addicts have sought "through prayer and meditation to improve our conscious contact with God as we understand Him, praying only for knowledge of His will for us and the power to carry that out."

In 1994, Koenig and his Duke University colleagues began a study of the relationship between religious practices and alcoholism among a large sample of adult Southerners. They found that (1) alcohol use and dependence were significantly lower among people who engaged in private worship (including prayer and scriptural study); (2) both recent and lifetime problems were lower among those who attended worship services; and (3) people who attended church at least weekly had one-third the rate of alcohol abuse of less frequent attenders.[15]

The National Institute for Healthcare Research convened an expert panel to review the reliability of data collected and published to date on spiritual and religious factors in substance abuse.[16] On the basis of a remarkably extensive literature accumulated over twenty years, the panel concluded that religious and spiritual involvement predicts less use of and fewer problems with alcohol, tobacco, and illicit drugs.[17] The panel confirmed that involvement with Alcoholics Anonymous is associated with better outcomes after outpatient treatment.[18] The evidence is strong that refocusing on spirituality is a primary means of recovery.

While substance abuse does make a mockery of the soul, some religions have assigned very circumscribed sacred uses of alcohol, peyote, and certain other drugs to supposedly induce religious experiences. The dominant traditional view, however, is that intoxication and spirituality are mutually exclusive.

Conversion experiences are associated with recovery from the powers of addiction.[19] (Yet those traditions in which such substances are deemed sacred nevertheless merit reasonable degrees of judicial and social tolerance.)

Mental Health

Meta-analysis of three decades of empirical studies in the social sciences indicates that spirituality is related to a variety of mental health outcomes, including subjective well-being, life satisfaction, and reduced rates of depression and suicide.[20] Although longitudinal studies yield similar results, these findings are based largely on cross-sectional data.[21] Religious faith has been shown to protect against serious stress in many groups, including bereaved parents, family caregivers of loved ones with dementia, and older African American males.[22]

Patients receiving religious psychotherapy show more rapid recovery from anxiety symptoms than do those receiving traditional secular therapy alone. A randomized study of sixty-two Muslim patients with generalized anxiety disorder indicated that those receiving psychotherapy and anxiolytic drugs, coupled with the use of prayer and the reading of verses from the Koran, clearly improved more quickly than those receiving psychotherapy and drugs alone.[23] A study of 128 African American persons with schizophrenia and their families indicates that these urban patients were less likely to be rehospitalized if their families encouraged them to continue religious worship while they were still in the hospital.[24] Another study found that depressed patients who had a strong intrinsic religious faith recovered 70 percent faster from depression than those with weaker faith.[25] Among thirty-three elderly women hospitalized with hip fractures, greater religiosity was associated with less depression and longer walking distances at the time of hospital discharge.[26]

Kenneth I. Pargament's text *The Psychology of Religion and Coping: Theory, Research, and Practice* is a powerful social scientific interpretation of all the data on spirituality and coping.[27] Psychiatric residency programs in the United States now require a curriculum on religion and spirituality in clinical practice, and major teaching modules have been developed.[28] It appears that *Homo religiosus* comes to the surface of human experience under conditions of stress. Thomas à Kempis understood this long ago in writing of the uses of adversity: "It is good for us to encounter troubles and adversities from time to time, for trouble often compels a man to search his own heart. It reminds him that he is in exile here, and that he can put his trust in nothing in this world."[29] Kempis describes a turning toward the Supreme Being that is intensified by adversity.

Religious coping with illness provides more favorable mental health outcomes than nonreligious coping behaviors.[30] Researchers at a conference entitled "The Roles of Religiousness and Spirituality in Rehabilitation and the Lives of Those with Disability," held at the National Institutes of Health in May 1995, concluded that spiritually based hope is the single most important variable in patient adjustment.[31] A 1993 survey conducted in an inpatient rehabilitation unit indicated that 74 percent of patients considered their religious and spiritual beliefs to be important, 54 percent desired pastoral counseling, 45 percent thought not enough attention was given to spiritual and religious beliefs, and a substantial 73 percent said that no one from the health care staff ever spoke to them about spiritual and religious concerns. Of most concern was that only 16 percent of the physicians on staff ever inquired about these concerns. The authors concluded that rehabilitation personnel, particularly the physician team leader, should be educated about the diversity of patients' religious beliefs and should address them more fully.[32]

Physical Illness

A number of longitudinal studies indicate a correlation between increased life expectancy and religiosity. The most significant study, conducted by William J. Strawbridge and colleagues, examined the relationship between mortality and attending religious services in 5,286 people aged twenty-one to sixty-five in Alameda County between 1965 and 1994.[33] The researchers analyzed questionnaire data procured at four intervals throughout the course of the study. This large and well-designed study, published in the *American Journal of Public Health,* indicated that regular religious attenders had an overall 23 percent reduced risk of dying in this twenty-eight–year period when compared with nonattenders. Other studies show reduced mortality following cardiac surgery among those receiving comfort and support from religion.[34] In another impressive study, also published in the prestigious *American Journal of Public Health,* 1,931 elderly residents of Marin County, California, were followed for a five-year period. Subjects were divided into two groups: "attenders" (including weekly and occasional) and "nonattenders."[35] Those who attended religious services were 36 percent less likely to die during this period. After controlling for certain variables (including age, sex, marital status, number of chronic diseases, lower body disability, balance problems, exercise, smoking status, alcohol use, weight, social support, and depression), persons attending religious services were 24 percent less likely to die during these five years.

Since the early 1990s, the epidemiology of religious influences on morbidity and health has become a significant area of scientific study.[36] A number of reliable studies indicate that religious commitment is associated with lower blood pressure.[37] Lower cancer mortality rates have been found in U.S. counties with high levels of religious group membership.[38] Religiousness appears to influence the timing of death around religious holidays.[39] It is a significant factor in reducing stress related to physical illness;[40] recovery from illness;[41] illness prevention;[42] prevention of heart disease;[43] mitigation of pain;[44] amelioration of suffering;[45] adjustment to disability;[46] timing of death;[47] and recovery from cardiac surgery in the elderly.[48] A useful summary of these and other data for family practitioners concludes that religion has a beneficial role in physical illness prevention, coping, and recovery.[49]

The emerging field of psychoneuroimmunology suggests that religious faith will inevitably have some health consequences.[50] Esther M. Sternberg's research is especially relevant in underscoring the connection between emotions and disease.[51] Internist Herbert Benson, president and founder of the Mind-Body Medical Institute at Harvard University, has reviewed three decades of literature on the impact of religious belief on physical health and illness.[52]

Research indicates that older adults who reside in deteriorated inner-city neighborhoods experience more physical health problems than do elderly persons living in better environments. Data from a nationwide longitudinal survey of elderly people indicate that the noxious impact of living in such neighborhoods on changes in self-rated health over time is offset for older adults who rely heavily on religious coping strategies. In other words, while physical health problems are generally increased in such environments, religious coping serves as a buffer.[53] This study encourages us to explore questions about the impact of religiosity on physical health.[54]

Death and Dying

Many (but not all) people with a terminal diagnosis appeal to some higher being in the universe who they believe might have greater control over their illness than they do.[55] All religious traditions provide interpretations and coping strategies to navigate this boundary of fragility and dying.[56] The hospice tradition provides the best example of a good dying because it combines pain relief, psychological and relational well-being, and pastoral-spiritual care.[57]

Even outside of hospice, few compassionate clinicians have forgotten about the place of spirituality in decisions about dying.[58] Physician-priests in Tibet, for example, have long used and prescribed meditative techniques for those with painful terminal illnesses.[59] It is not surprising that meditation has also been used among thanatologists in many hospice settings to enhance terminal care. In the West, meditation and prayer were once an integral part of the normative "art of dying," taught by Judaism and Christianity throughout the Middle Ages and the Renaissance.[60]

Pain is a complex, multidimensional psychological state with affective and sensory features; suffering is experienced as a threat to the integrity of the self that results in the exhaustion of psychosocial and personal resources for coping.[61] Because spirituality is an integral part of most patients' personal coping resources,[62] it is essential that it be appreciated by physicians; neglect of this dimension must be taken seriously and should at least be considered poor medical practice.

Consider, for example, the phenomenon of human hope. Hope is an aspect of spiritual well-being that concerns dimensions of possibility and confidence in future outcomes, whether probable or improbable. It has been studied in cancer patients,[63] and in patients with AIDS.[64] Hope is important to patients with terminal or chronic diagnoses and should fall within the clinical concerns of the skilled physician. In times of severe disabling injury, hope ("the passion for the possible") may be mediated through ritual, meditation, prayer, traditional sacred narratives, or other inspirational readings. A team of psychiatric researchers using positron emission tomography has demonstrated cerebral neurobiological correlates with hope and hopelessness.[65]

Bereavement is of obvious relevance. In a study of Islamic patients, bereaved persons were placed in two groups. One group was given support for religious beliefs, along with standard psychotherapeutic assistance; the second group was given only the latter. The group whose belief systems were supported did much better.[66] The secular medicalization of bereavement support, which emerged after World War II in the United States, has recognized the role of emotional sequencing and the need for standard psychiatric medical treatment. It is ironic, then, that a religiously appreciative model would enhance outcomes in treating the grief reaction.[67]

Having summarized only some of the stronger studies on the human inclination toward a Creative Presence in the contexts of substance abuse, mental health, physical health, and death and dying, I turn now to the context of dementia and offer some fresh data. Few illnesses are more aptly described as limit situations than a diagnosis of progressive dementia, for this is a disease that will eventually strip away the story of one's life, consigning the self to the pure present as the temporal glue between past, present, and future is irreversibly dissolved.

The Context of Dementia

The Place of Spirituality in the Lives of Patients

Consider Oliver Sacks's compelling description of a patient with severe Korsakov's dementia. Sacks observed: "Seeing Jim in the chapel opened my eyes to other realms where the soul is called on, and held, and stilled, in attention and communion. The same depth of absorption and attention was to be seen in relation to music and art: he had no difficulty."[68] Sacks goes further regarding Jim: "But if he was held in emotional and spiritual attention—in the contemplation of nature or art, in listening to music, in taking part in the Mass in chapel—the attention, its 'mood', its quietude, would persist for a while, and there would be in him a pensiveness and peace we rarely, if ever saw during the rest of his life at the Home."[69] Without asserting the existence of a soul that lies beneath the confusion of dementia, Sacks does assert "the undiminished possibility of reintegration by art, by communion, by touching the human spirit: and this can be preserved in what seems at first a hopeless state of neurological devastation."[70]

When informed of a diagnosis of Alzheimer's disease (AD), how might a person find meaning and a degree of inner peace in the midst of anxiety? The person must navigate a journey into deep forgetfulness, which seems only slightly less anxiety-producing when one forgets that one forgets. Caregivers, in turn, may be shaken to their spiritual foundations by unexpected responsibilities.

Chaplains should have a significant role in the disclosure of a diagnosis as serious as AD. They must be able to encourage hope despite the perils of forgetfulness. Hope can address secular matters, such as future plans and relationships, or religious matters of ultimate destiny, such as resurrection. Hope is an aspect of religious well-being. Preservation of hope can maximize a patient's psychological adjustment to a severe disability such as dementia. The spiritual history of patients can be very useful in understanding their sources of well-being and in helping them to identify religious resources in the community. Clinicians should not only acknowledge the importance of spirituality and religion in diagnosed individuals and refer those individuals to clergy but also respond (if willing) to the patient's requests for spirituality in the physician-patient relationship. This last item is a possibility only upon patient request.

One of the finest autobiographical accounts of living with the diagnosis and initial decline of AD is Rev. Robert Davis's *My Journey into Alzheimer's Disease*. He writes as follows:

> One night in Wyoming, as I lay in a motel crying out to my Lord, my long desperate prayers were suddenly answered. As I lay there in the blackness silently shrieking out my often repeated prayer, there was suddenly a light that seemed to fill my very soul. The sweet, holy presence of Christ came to me. He spoke to my spirit and said, "Take my peace. Stop your struggling. It is all right. This is all in keeping with my will for your life. . . . Lie back in your Shepherd's arms, and take my peace."[71]

As Rev. Davis "mourned the loss of old abilities," he nevertheless could draw on his Christianity: "I choose to take things moment by moment, thankful for everything that I have, instead of raging wildly at the things that I have lost."[72] Yet as he struggled to find a degree of peace amidst decline, he was also keenly aware of people who "simply cannot handle being around someone who is mentally and emotionally impaired."[73] The journey was made more navigable in his church community and through the love of his wife.

People with a diagnosis of AD often pray, for they cling to whatever faith they have in the meaningful and beneficent purposes underlying the universe. They pray because the routine and the control have been taken from their lives and probably because they fear the future. They are shaken existentially and must begin a final phase of their journey in remarkable trust. The person with a diagnosis of AD will often desire to pray with family members, in religious communities, and alone. The word *prayer* comes from the Latin *precari,* "to entreat," or to ask earnestly. It comes from the same root as the word *precarious,* and it is in the precariousness of emerging forgetfulness that the person with dementia is often driven to prayer. Chaplains and clinicians should encourage this propensity to gain strength through prayer in the midst of cognitive decline.

An autobiographical account from my earlier book demonstrates the search for meaning typified by persons with dementia.[74] The following story—only lightly edited—was told by a woman in her mid-forties with dementia, etiology unknown. She is conversant, although there are some days when she is too mentally confused to engage in much dialogue. She has more difficulty responding to open-ended questions but does very well if her conversation partner cues her by mentioning several alternative words from which she might choose, at which point she can be quite articulate:

> It was just about this time three years ago that I recall laughing with my sister while in dance class at my turning the big 40. "Don't worry, life begins at forty," she exclaimed, and then sweetly advised her younger sister of all the wonders in life still to be found. Little did either of us realize what a cruel twist life was proceeding to take. It was a fate neither she nor I ever imagined someone in our age group could encounter.
>
> Things began to happen that I just couldn't understand. There were times I addressed friends by the wrong name. Comprehending conversations seemed almost impossible. My attention span became quite short. Notes were needed to remind me of things to be done and how to do them. I would slur my speech, use inappropriate words, or simply eliminate one from a sentence. This caused not only frustration for me, but also a great deal of embarrassment. Then came the times I honestly could not remember how to plan a meal or shop for groceries.
>
> One day, while out for a walk on my usual path in a city in which I had resided for 11 years, nothing looked

familiar. It was as if I was lost in a foreign land, yet I had the sense to ask for directions home.

There were more days than not when I was perfectly fine; but to me, they did not make up for the ones that weren't. I knew there was something terribly wrong and after 18 months of undergoing a tremendous amount of tests and countless visits to various doctors, I was proven right.

Dementia is the disease, they say, cause unknown. At this point it no longer mattered to me just what that cause was because the tests eliminated the reversible ones, my hospital coverage was gone, and my spirit was too worn to even care about the name of something irreversible.

I was angry. I was broken and this was something I could not fix, nor to date can anyone fix it for me. How was I to live without myself? I wanted her back!

She was a strong and independent woman. She always tried so hard to be a loving wife, a good mother, a caring friend and a dedicated employee. She had self-confidence and enjoyed life. She never imagined that by the age of 41 she would be forced into retirement. She had not yet observed even one of her sons graduate from college, nor known the pleasures of a daughter-in-law, nor held a grandchild in her arms.

Needless to say, the future did not look bright. The leader must now learn to follow. Adversities in life were once looked upon as a challenge; now they're just confusing situations that someone else must handle. Control of *my life* will slowly be relinquished to others. I must learn to trust— completely.

An intense fear enveloped my entire being as I mourned the loss of what was and the hopes and dreams that might never be. How could this be happening to me? What exactly will become of me? These questions occupied much of my time for far too many days.

Then one day as I fumbled around the kitchen to pre-
pare a pot of coffee, something caught my eye through the
window. It had snowed and I had truly forgotten what a
beautiful sight a soft, gentle snowfall could be. I eagerly
but so slowly dressed and went outside to join my son,
who was shoveling our driveway. As I bent down to gather
a mass of those radiantly white flakes on my shovel, it
seemed as though I could do nothing but marvel at their
beauty. Needless to say, he did not share in my enthusiasm;
to him it was a job, but to me it was an experience.

Later I realized that, for a short period of time, God
granted me the ability to see a snowfall through the same
innocent eyes of the child I once was, so many years ago. I
am still here, I thought, and there will be wonders to be
held in each new day; they are just different now. . . . Now
my quality of life is feeding the dogs, looking at flowers.
My husband says I am more content now than ever before!
Love and dignity, those are the keys. This brings you back
down to the basics in life, a smile makes you happy.

People with AD, as well as their caregivers, can benefit remarkably from pastoral care. Sometimes the patient who has
not spoken coherently for several years will suddenly blurt
out a prayer or a hymn, for such deeply learned material is
the very last to disappear. The beauty of litanies, prayers, and
hymns has a certain affective power. I remain open to the idea
that, as the capacity for technical (means to ends) rationality
fades, more contemplative and spiritual capacities are elevated.
Demented people continue to respond to their faith and inner
needs through long-remembered rituals that connect them
with the present. Prayers and hymns are still familiar in many
cases, especially after several repetitions.

In September 1998 I facilitated, with the help of Cleveland
Area Chapter of the Alzheimer's Association, a focus group to

explore religiosity with AD-diagnosed persons in the mild stage of the disease. The following are representative transcriptions from this three-hour session.

Case 1: Bunny
Sally (the group's moderator) asks Bunny if she prays now that she has a diagnosis of AD. Bunny responds:

> Well I never say it out loud but I do it in the car, you know, when I've been frustrated I will call for the Lord to help me do, you know, what I should do and not be angry some-times. And I think it's hard on the people that I live with to have to put up with me sometimes because I can't remem-ber anything. And so, I pray silently to myself. (p. 2)

Bunny continues describing her reliance on the Lord and her now consistent attendance at her Presbyterian church.

Case 2: Peter
Sally asks Peter to describe his experience with his diagnosis. Peter states: "Oh, I was devastated that I lost the technical ability to do my job, and the sense of pride that comes into play. And I think pride sometimes is an evil factor because it weighs on your mind and it tells you that you are worthless and it kind of destroys your self-worth" (p. 5). Peter goes to his Roman Catholic church every Sunday and reads daily from a prayer book:

> It's a daily prayer book and each day of the week—like Monday, Tuesday—it has a prayer. And every morning when I wake up I read the prayer for that particular day. And, like I say, before when I was working, I would never read any-thing like this. You know, it was the farthest thing from my

mind. But now every morning I read it faithfully. Monday's prayer I happen to like most because it kind of applies to us here. Happy disease? It says, my Lord God, I do not see the road ahead of me. I cannot know for certain where it will end. I know that you will lead me by the right road, though I might know nothing about it. Therefore, I trust you always. I will not fear. For you are with me and you will never leave me to face my perils alone. And this gives me a sense of reassurance. (p. 6)

In the above lines, Peter states that his interest in such prayers did not exist prior to his diagnosis with AD. Indeed, his dementia brings with it something like a conversion experience:

I'd say, why did you [the Lord] let this happen to me? I had such a good career. Everything was going fine for me. He would say to you probably, "Well, why did you fight it? I was trying to lead you in this direction." Oh, I didn't realize that. Well, I've come to the conclusion that everything has a purpose so the Good Lord, he knows the best for you. So maybe this was to slow me down to enjoy life and to enjoy my family and to enjoy what's out there. And right now, I can say that I'm a better person for it in appreciation to other people's needs and illnesses than I ever was when I was working that rat race back and forth day to day. (p. 7)

Peter emphasizes his volunteer work riding in a van, making sure that the elder care center participants keep their seat belts on and get out of the van without falling. "Oh, yes," he adds, "like I say, to give yourself and volunteer and help other people means a lot" (p. 9).

As it turns out, Peter's turn to religion in the midst of early AD was precipitated by a singular event:

And I had a vision when I was sleeping one time. And this vision was I was at work and I was a technician and I was out in the field doing my job on this gas meter that takes a sample of the gas and I was at the meter and I saw this bright light to the left of me and I turned and I looked and I was kind of scared and then I looked to my right and there was a bright light there. And then I heard this voice say, "Don't worry, everything will be all right. I will take care of you." And from that day on, I woke up and I said, I'm going to accept this disease. And my wife says my goodness, you've changed, you know. I said that I was going to accept this [AD] and live with it and go on from here and enjoy my life. And I think it was. . . . Some people might say it was just a vision or a dream or something. But it put everything in perspective for me, and, from that point on, I have been more calm, more caring and everything has just seemed to fall in place. (p. 5)

Peter, incidentally, has worked for most of his adult life as a technician for the East Ohio Gas Company. His visionary dream was clearly a turning point in his emotional adjustment to the losses he was experiencing: "I used to have emotional breakdowns where we [Peter and wife] were crying and upset and that's all been gone. I don't get emotional anymore. And I even think the memory has kind of leveled off. It's a very calming effect" (p. 9).

Peter's wife testifies that his emotional state did indeed change after the visionary dream experience. From then on, he was both intensely religious and also more altruistic than he ever had been in the past. The depth of Peter's experience is equal to many recorded by eminent psychologists of religion, and his life transformation follows the contours of religious experience described earlier. Remarkably, all of this happened to a man who had received an otherwise devastating diagnosis of a disease that will eventually rob him of self-identity and the temporal connections between past, present, and future.[75]

Suffice it to state that religious coping with this diagnosis is widespread, if not ubiquitous. Our focus group informants were not selected for any reason of religiosity and were not all as pronounced in their experience as was Peter. However, all resorted to prayer and religious ideation as their chief matrix for hope.

The Place of Spirituality in the Lives of Caregivers

The vast majority of humankind prays for the sick. This is clearly the case with family members caring for loved ones with AD. In a recent study of religiosity variables in relation to perceived caregiver rewards, African American women caring for elderly persons with major deficits in activities of daily living perceived greater benefits when their caring was based on a spiritual-religious reframing of their situation. Religiosity indicators (i.e., "prayer, comfort from religion, self-rated religiosity, attendence at religious services") were especially significant as coping resources in African American women caregivers.[76] Because religiosity is a clear stress deterrent, it also affects depression rates, which are extraordinarily high in AD caregivers. These authors suggest that "if religiosity indicators are shown to enhance a caregiver's perceived rewards, health care professionals could encourage caregivers to use their religiosity to reduce the negative consequences and increase the rewards of caregiving." [77] This seems self-evident.

Other studies indicate that religiosity is an important factor in coping with the sometimes relentless stress induced by caring for someone with AD.[78] In a study by Peter V. Rabins et al., thirty-two family caregivers of persons with AD and thirty caregivers of persons with cancer were compared cross-sectionally. The study attempted to determine whether the type of illness affected the emotional state of the caregiver, as well as to identify correlates of both undesirable and desirable emotional outcomes. While no prominent differences were found between the two groups, correlates of negative and positive emotional status were identified—for example, caregiver personality variables, number of social supports, and the feeling that one is supported by one's religious faith. Specifically, "emotional distress was predicted by self-reported low or absent religious faith."[79] Moreover, religiosity predicted positive emotional states in caregiving. Interestingly, the study suggests that it was "belief, rather than social contact, that was important."[80]

In another study, the spiritual perspectives of seventeen caregiver wives of dementia victims and twenty-three noncaregiving wives of healthy adults were compared in a pilot study using a convenience sample. Caregiver wives used symbols, such as God, and spiritual behaviors, such as prayer and forgiveness, as coping mechanisms. Caregivers tended to share the problems and joys of living according to their spiritual beliefs more often than the noncaregiver wives of healthy adults. Caregivers also engaged in private prayer and sought spiritual guidance in making decisions in their everyday lives more often.[81] Both these studies point to the central importance of spirituality and religion in caregiving.[82]

The reader may remain skeptical of anecdotal focus group information around dementia, but many of the studies cited above are quantitative and impressive. If spirituality and religion become so important in this and the other illness contexts described above, then perhaps Jaspers was in fact correct in arguing that limit situations free us to more fully express our evolved spiritual and religion inclinations. If this is the case, we must briefly raise the question of a correlative right to religious expression in the health care setting.

Free Religious Expression in Health Care

The pluralistic and social scientific study of the impact of patient spirituality is very different from the theological enterprise of the seminary.[83] Physicians should be aware of the growing numbers of studies that demonstrate the value of spirituality as a coping mechanism for patients with major illness.[84] The attention given in medical education to patient spirituality and religious belief is another indication of clinical relevance.[85] Focused volumes of specialty journals have recently been devoted to the spiritual or religious factors in illness coping.[86]

Physicians must do more than tolerate the meaning-giving belief systems of their patients. It is these belief systems that provide hope, security, meaning, and strength to empower patients to cope with the shattering experience of severe illness.[87] Physicians should be concerned with the social, scientific, and historical understanding of the empowering presence of spirituality (often, but not necessarily, embedded in a religious tradition) in the patient's experience of illness, rather than with its essential validity or truth.[88] The importance of patient beliefs is exemplified in historical accounts of healers who possess knowledge of both medicine and spirituality.[89]

A study of 203 family practice adult inpatients at sites in urban Kentucky and eastern North Carolina indicated that 77 percent wanted physicians to consider their spiritual needs, 37 percent wanted physicians to discuss these needs with them more frequently, and a somewhat surprising 48 percent wanted their physicians to pray with them. Regrettably, 68 percent said that their physicians never discussed religious beliefs with them.[90] Why is this? Part of the reason may be that there has been an artificial separation between the domains of traditional allopathic medical practice and spirituality. The arena of spiritual counseling has been reserved for those with special training, such as chaplains or pastoral counselors. It is this separation that drives so many Americans toward alternative medicine practitioners and, in some cases, away from proven and optimal allopathic treatments.

It is possible, of course, that the above study and others like it are skewed because they were conducted in a region of the country in which people tend to be overtly religious. Would the same study yield the same results in New York City, San Francisco, or London? Extrapolating from any study with such a restricted database is of marginal value. However, the studies cited across the literature indicate a pervasive spiritual-religious tendency in circumstances of severe illness.

Physician training may be a more important factor in this neglect of the spiritual-religious aspect of patients. In the last three decades, medicine has made significant technological advances, all of which had to be incorporated into curricula. As a result, it has been noted that young doctors may be excellent diagnosticians and technicians but still lack the humanitarian skills required to be compassionate caregivers who can communicate effectively with their patients about preferences for treatment, prognoses, lifestyles, beliefs, fears, and hopes. A critical part of this communication is the ability to discuss a patient's spiritual beliefs and how these affect his or her health.

Inquiry about patient spirituality can certainly be incorporated into either the social or past life history of the patient. One study indicates that very few patients are offended by gentle, nonjudgmental questioning about such matters; in many cases, they are much more willing to explore plans for a good dying in the context of their beliefs.[91] In another study, 40 percent of patients welcomed the idea of having their physicians explore religious issues with them, especially in the contexts of major life events (e.g., birth, death, major surgery, major illness, and terminal illness).[92] In the same study, physicians reported the extent to which patients asked them spiritual-religious questions as occasional (77 percent), frequent (10 percent), and never (12 percent).

Again, to be unsupportive of the spirituality of coping is a patent violation of the principle of beneficence. For example, a recent empirical study indicates that women with gynecologic cancer depend upon their religious convictions and experiences as they cope with the disease.[93] For the oncologist to be ignorant or unappreciative of this fact could easily result in neglect or harm to patients, including adverse physical consequences. Some initial conversation about spiritual concerns is imperative in order to make necessary referrals to pastoral care.[94]

Patient Rights to Religious Expression and
Subsequent Pastoral Care

The growing extent of the data supporting the benefits of spirituality and religion to patients coping with illness mandates that patients be allowed to freely express their spirituality in a respectful and supportive clinical environment. Of course, even without such data, free expression in this area can be adequately justified on the principle of *respect for patient autonomy*. In turn, all physicians should be able to discuss a patient's spiritual concerns in a respectful manner when requested by the patient. The physician should always respect the patient's privacy regarding matters of spirituality and religion and should never impose his or her beliefs on patients.

Physicians often suggest that patients exercise or quit smoking. Given the data on beneficial health outcomes, should physicians also encourage spiritual and religious practices? Of course, physicians can encourage spiritual and religious practices for those whose belief systems incorporate these values. It would be disrespectful, not beneficial, and not supportive of autonomy to tell a patient with no spiritual beliefs to "get" some.

Referrals to chaplains are critical to good health care practice and are as appropriate as referrals to other specialists.[95] Because physicians do not routinely inquire about spirituality and do not appreciate its importance, however, referrals to chaplains are woefully inadequate.[96] For example, there is a need for formal linkage between clergy and mental health professionals in order to enhance therapeutic efficacy with patients of various religious traditions.[97] There is also a need for a developed linkage between clinical ethics (in which most formal education, theory, and practice are inattentive to spirituality) and a chaplaincy awakened to the important role that religion has in allowing patients and families to broach matters of death and dying. Chaplains should be integral to all health care teams.

One poll found that a full 64 percent of Americans think that doctors should join their patients in prayer if the patient requests this.[98] There is wide recognition of a "religiosity gap" between patients and physicians that limits therapeutic efficacy.[99] Yet in 1995 the *Wall Street Journal* reported that a Brown University professor asserted: "If my doctor prayed for my recovery, I'd consider a malpractice suit."[100] Significant numbers of Americans are not interested in having their doctors discuss spirituality and religion because of a deep-rooted and time-honored American resistance to religious coercion. The imposition of spirituality must always be avoided. There is, however, also a time-honored American commitment to freedom of religious expression that is ensconced in the words of the First Amendment religion clause, "nor prohibiting the freedom thereof." This freedom applies to patients, and it should not be transgressed. Thirty-seven percent of patients in one study indicated a desire to have their physicians pray with them.[101] The skillful clinician must know when and how to address these desires.

The role of religion in sickness is remarkable. It is a strange and intractable occurrence in human history that correlates with the first primitive experiences of religious awe. We see an emergent human drive toward a Creative Presence exhibited most profoundly and widely in severe illness and dying; sometimes this drive is petitionary, and sometimes it is purely contemplative. There is a heightened sense of the fullness of Being. Because it seems so ubiquitously natural across cultures and epochs, this instinct for and dependence on the Supreme Being must provide some evolutionary selective advantage.

The extent of spirituality and religion in severe illness defines us human beings. In times of plague, pestilence, war, and natural disaster, the innumerable false personas (a word derived from the Latin for "mask") that we develop to play the game of life are abruptly ripped off our faces. (In Western religious thought, the catastrophic is often couched in the images of a final battle between good and evil, judgment, and apocalypse.)

When, however, the end-time comes in our own lives, and when our brains or bodies begin to deteriorate and die, we are clearly dealing with realities. Here is the final existential battle of life, and it is ultimately a lost cause. Then the masks that we wear to play roles in the game of life become useless, and the drive toward a Creative Presence is revealed.

The Objective Study of the Religious Nature of Humankind in the Clinical Context

In April 1995, a conference entitled "Spiritual Dimensions in Clinical Research" was sponsored by the National Institute for Healthcare Research. A dozen leading clinical empirical researchers presented papers on methodological issues, and the conference was reported in the *Journal of the American Medical Association*.[102] In several presentations and audience responses, cases were described in which Institutional Review Boards (IRBs) at prestigious academic medical research institutions had refused to approve social scientific research on religion and spirituality. The assumption was that these topics were unsuited for scientific investigation.

Scientific freedom to study religion and health should not be violated by IRBs. Critical intelligence requires that this inquiry must be pluralistic—that is, attentive to religious diversity and objective in the sense of being based on good scientific methodology. Neglecting the study of religion and health may result in less than optimal patient care. There can be little respect for the patient's religiosity unless the clinician has some data indicating its potential significance. Yet religious attitudes in the patient, a powerful dynamic, are sometimes dismissed from scientific measurement. Without a more holistic view of the human person, allopathic medicine, for all its technological sophistication, loses patients to alternative practitioners.

The problem of setting aside the study of religion has historical roots. We have inherited a Western view of the person that has been shaped by struggles for ascendency between scientific views and historical theologies. Because this divorce demands the staking out of territory and defense of ground gained, clinicians can be indifferent to theological and religious values, if not confrontational. In some areas of health care, the result is a polarization between professionals and those in need of care.

Given the dramatic success of empirical science in biomedicine, medicine can now afford to apply the scientific method to the religious dimension of human experience without risking embarrassment or diminution of power. The scientific method must be free of either sacred or secular ideological interference in its interpretation of the facts, even if perfectly objective interpretation is impossible. Instead, interference is now manifested as an antireligious positivist ideology that condemns the scientific study of religion in health.

Any confessional study of theological beliefs and traditions is fitting for departments of theology, for such study makes no claim to scientific objectivity. Religious studies, however, do seek objectivity. The objective empirical method has been applied to religion by sociologists, historians, psychologists, anthropologists, and political scientists, including Max Weber, Emile Durkheim, Ernst Troeltsch, Joachim Wach, Wilhelm Wundt, Erik Erikson, Claude Levi-Strauss, Victor Turner, and Mircea Eliade. Religion began to move into the academic mainstream in the 1960s, when secular colleges and universities began to set up new departments of religious studies. This emergence was in part due to the continued widespread interest in religion. Yet some are still unable to draw the simple distinction between studying religion and teaching people to be religious. As Ninian Smart, a leading scholar in comparative religions, writes, "To the historians and social scientists I say: We can let you hear more clearly the sound of symbols. To the atheists I say: The exploration of the power of world views is compatible with everything you stand for, and everything which you oppose. To the pious I say: It is your decision to be pious, our task is analysis and synthesis"[103] It is possible that the most objective study of the facts will eventually demonstrate the plausibility of faith.

Religious facts should be understood as a part of health and health care research because they are so elemental and so pervasive in the experience of illness. Ignoring these facts can only reduce the person affected by illness to a secular existentialist image of the self. Religion is universal. Some cultures are entirely dominated by it; in none is it entirely absent; in illness it is nearly ubiquitous. Thus, the competent study of religion in health care should need no defense and should be encouraged by funding agencies, including the public National Institutes of Health. Without such study, entire generational cohorts of professionals will be denied knowledge that is essential to effective patient care. Although religious beliefs may be deemed by skeptics as more myth than fact or more aberrant than normal, they can be obscured only by ideology in the most negative sense of the word—that is, the systematic and unscientific denial of those empirical facts that one simply refuses to consider.

The American experiment in liberty confers respect and rights upon the religious individual. By dishonoring the religious factor through ignorance, caregivers violate a sphere of freedom of expression and experience that lies at the core of our political heritage. By discriminating against the study of religion, we limit our ability to speak publicly about it; as a result, patients are easily misunderstood and, in various ways, denied full therapeutic empathy. We impose a climate of secularism and irreligion on persons who are predictably *Homo religiosus*. We do them a grave disservice.

Concluding Reflections

Some critics of this chapter might argue that all these spiritual-religious findings reveal only delusions that give false comfort. They might be, in Sartrean language, instances of "bad faith." Such perspectives can be well argued, but they are ultimately reductive. To claim that such experiences are "nothing but" the creations of anxiety is to go beyond what the data fairly allow. The assertion that these experiences are nothing but delusions is itself dogmatic and counterintuitive, particularly in light of the preponderance of spiritual-religious expression in such limit situations over the course of history and cultures. Cross-cultural studies generally underscore this hypothesis.[104] Even in an ardently secular European country such as Sweden, where only 2 percent of the population reports weekly church attendance, a majority of cancer patients report that comfort from religious beliefs is important to them.[105] All that can be concluded is that being religious seems to confer a selective advantage in coping. If religious beliefs, experiences, and practices do assist with coping in catastrophic scenarios, protect against suicide and depression, and even confer other possible benefits, then persons with the capacity for religious experience have a consequent selective advantage over others; eventually, they will dominate the population pool by evolutionary laws. The ubiquity of religious behavior across culture and time suggests in and of itself that some benefits must exist.

CHAPTER TWO

The Religious Inclination: An Emerging Neuroscientific Objectivity

The preceding chapter highlighted the extent and significance of religious expression in time of illness, a context that is representative of the wider category of limit situations. There are surely other examples worth studying, such as times of war, oppression, betrayal, and any other situations in which we rightly perceive the limitations of our own powers to shape and control the course of events. It is said, for instance, that there are no atheists in foxholes, although there are surely some. The religious inclination is important in the way that we handle severe levels of suffering, failure, illness, risk, and disappointment.

Any human inclination includes a central neurological pathway, for the brain is the locus of mentation, orientation, emotion, and perception. It is thus reasonable to ask if the spiritual and religious inclination is "hard-wired" in the brain, and if it is, the implication must be that it is a permanent and distinguishing feature of the human creature. This chapter reviews current thinking in what has come to be widely known as "neurotheology." How can we begin to understand the Augustinian "thirst" for God in the light of brain science?

There is a metaphysical subtext. Does this capacity point toward some objective higher entity in the universe? Animals evolved the capacity to breathe air because oxygen surrounds them; they evolved the capacity to hear because sound exists; they evolved the capacity to see because there is an environment to be seen. As earlier stated, it is plausible to surmise that human beings evolved the capacity to experience God because God exists and confers some benefits, including comfort and serenity in difficult times. Plausibility does not imply proven fact or compelling logic, but it does preclude ruling something out as untenable.

Just because we perceive something does not make it real; it could be the figment of the imagination. But evolutionarily, our complex minds seem to lean toward God so pervasively that it is difficult to reduce this to imagination, and it is unlikely that the economy of evolution would have them leaning toward nothing. This assertion has slight resonance with the classical ontological argument for the existence of God: we are able to think of God, and therefore God exists. I hold that the fact of our common reliance on God plausibly indicates that there is a God to be relied on; otherwise, it is unlikely that we would have evolved this remarkable capacity. The human brain is, on the other hand, capable of every sort of illusion, for which corrective medications are now often available. But the persistent and beneficial human reliance on God is neither dysfunctional or peculiar in most instances, and therefore the neurological pathways that make this reliance possible are not deemed pathological. The question is whether such complex pathways need to be lured into existence by an evolutionarily attractive ultimate reality of divine love, a position I hold as a matter of Christian faith rather than strict logic. I will not ponder this much further, however, because even in the absence of God as an objective reality, the very fact that so many people indicate that they perceive God indicates that this tendency runs deep in human nature.

The Neuroscience of Spiritual and Religious Experience

Significant attention is being given to the neurological study of spiritual and religious experience in all its variations. What goes on neurologically in deep prayer, meditation, religious chanting, ritual, and the like? The religious traditions of the world all speak of some common experience of profound release from the cares and occupations of daily living, of a "letting go" of self, of an alleviation of fear and anxiety coupled with the emergence of a sense of inner peace, and of a renewing sense of connection with the universe and with others that is associated with divine love. The Dalai Lama, for instance, places the origins of compassionate love in this transformative experience, which is then, he contends, the deeper foundation of all active moral idealism (compassionate love) as well as moral minimalism (non-maleficence).[1] St. Augustine maintains that we are made to receive God, that in the absence of this reception we are restless and incomplete, that only through such spiritual experience can we achieve humility and release from egoism, and that all true joy and genuinely motivated love for one's neighbor emerge from this experience. In its longing for God, Augustine wrote, the human soul "thirsts like a land parched with drought, for just as it cannot give light to itself, neither can it quench its own thirst."[2] Inner peace and the overcoming of anger seem to be a key part of this spiritual experience, and only with this reordering of the self does the higher manifestation of ethical life become possible.

In the words of the Anglican mystic Evelyn Underhill,

> [I]t is only when the secret thirst of our whole being is thus re-ordered by God and set towards God, that peace is established in the house of life. Then the disorderly energies of emotion and will are rectified and harmonized, and all the various and wide-spreading *love* which we pour out

towards other souls and things is deepened, *unselfed* and made safe; because that which is now sought and loved in them is the imminent Divine thought and love.[3]

The question is this: How can we gain some neurological insight into these mysterious sorts of experiences, which are so widely and perennially reported across cultures?

The sense of alleviated anxiety and absence of fear may be associated with a dampening of the amygdala, the part of the interior brain where the emotional sense of fear ("fight or flight response") is located; the sense of oneness with the universe may rest in the quieting of parietal-lobe circuits, where spatial-temporal orientation and differentiation of self and world are based.[4] Single photon emission computed tomography (SPECT) allows the blood flow in the brain to be traced photographically. Andrew Newberg and his team of researchers at the University of Pennsylvania indicate that when a subject is having a spiritual experience based on meditation and deep prayer there is increased activity in the prefrontal cortex (associated with attentiveness), associated with a sense of peace, and a decreased activity in the superior parietal lobe (orientation to space and time), leading to a sense of cosmic unity. The middle temporal lobe is also active and is associated with the emotional aspects of spiritual experience such as joy and awe.[5]

Religious experiences have to do with "our limited personal relations with the transcendent Other which we call divine, eternal, or real" appearing perpetually.[6] Underhill synthesized descriptions of such experiences and ultimately identified three common key elements. First, there is the sense of profound security, "of being safely held in the cosmos of which, despite all contrary appearance, peace is the very heart, and which cannot be inimical to our true interests."[7] Second, "the relationship is felt [...] as the intimate and reciprocal communion of a person with a Person; a form of apprehension which is common to the great majority of devout nature."[8] And last, there is the perception of "inflowing power, a veritable accession of vitality."[9] Underhill speaks of a perennial "ineradicable impulse to transcendence"; this impulse, she adds, is most commonly expressed in the sense of a "quiet being with."[10]

Some persons may have an especially developed or sensitive neurological basis for spiritual and religious experience, or perhaps it is simply that they throw up fewer obstacles against it. Ordinary religiosity such as deep worship can, on a less dramatic level, involve aspects of the brain that are more intensely active in the religious genius.[11] Humans could still be very early in the process of developing the capacity to know the Creative Presence directly. Fully adequate knowledge is probably impossible. If our knowledge of this Presence were ever to be—that is, equal to its object—we would be equal to or even greater than that Presence. We would be putting the Creative Presence in our vest pockets, so to speak. Epistemological humility is in order—mystery remains.

A panel of neuroscientists convened to assess the current status of research on religious capacity. After providing an overview of research on physiologic and neurologic responses associated with common spiritual practices, neuropathological disorders, and pharmacological activation of "profound" spiritual experiences, they concluded that an impressive but embryonic neuroscience of religious experience exists. Moreover, the neuroscientists stated the following:

> Eventually, a neuroscience of spiritual experience will develop into a multidisciplinary approach with implications for neurobiology, physiology, mind/body medicine, physical and mental health, and perhaps even implications for theology and philosophy. But most importantly, the process must proceed with rigor and caution to sustain immutable scientific integrity.[12]

As in any new field of study, methodology is only unfolding.

The human brain is remarkably complex, with as many neuronal connections as there are stars in the universe. Perhaps much of religious experience correlates with the right side of the neocortex, which is said to be the locus of meaning seeking, although the science of left brain and right brain function is in the process of revision. Future brain-scanning studies may indicate brain correlates in experiencing a Creative Presence. Eugene d'Aquili and Andrew B. Newberg have gone farthest in mapping the functions of the brain and then suggesting how the brain is involved in mystical experiences with regard to both structure and biological mechanisms.[13] Yet it must be stated that all hypotheses regarding brain involvement remain preliminary at this time.

Neither d'Aquili nor Newberg wishes to argue firmly that the way in which the brain is set up for spiritual and religious experience has clear metaphysical implications. Similarly, William James did not argue that his lengthy compendium of religious experience demonstrated the existence of God. But James did, at the end of his *Varieties of Religious Experience,* conclude tentatively that some "More" exists and that across time and culture our connections with it lead to altruistic and loving behavior.[14] D'Aquili and Newberg hint in a similar direction but do not wish to be conclusive.

We turn now to several specific areas where neuroscience research has addressed spiritual and religious experience with some significant success, although it must be said that knowledge is only beginning to progress.

Near-Death Experiences

The possibility of a brain correlate for religious experience has been studied in near-death experiences (NDEs), which occur in about a third of people who come close to dying.[15] First described as a clinical syndrome in 1892, accounts of NDE exist widely across European, Middle Eastern, African, Indian, East Asian, Pacific, and Native American cultures, suggesting a neurological feature common to human beings, admixed with varied cultural perspectives.[16] Persons who have had an NDE usually report a panoramic life review.[17] Feelings of tranquility, love, destiny, and mortality acceptance are described as the affective dimension of the NDE, all of which are substantive aspects of religious experience.[18] The NDE has been interpreted with the help of neurobiological models that focus on neurotransmitters (including serotonin) and neuroanatomical loci. The extent of hard neuroscience done on NDE is impressive, although no brain pathway hypothesis has been clearly established. But NDE is "hypothetically localized in the limbic lobe."[19] This hypothesis does not imply that the NDE can be fully explained as nothing but a brain state, for there is no reason to think that the Supreme Being would not act on the limbic system in comforting the dying. As Bruce Greyson writes, "Correlating a brain state with an experience does not necessarily imply that brain states cause the experience; the brain state may simply reflect or allow the experience."[20]

Temporal-Lobe Epilepsy

For many decades, persons have described their subjective states just prior to an epileptic seizure in terms remarkably similar to descriptions of mystical religious experiences. This does not imply that all persons who have such experiences are undiagnosed temporal-lobe epileptics, although epilepsy suggests the sort of brain state that mystics claim as their own.[21] Epilepsy involves the temporal lobe in most instances, including the underlying limbic structures such as the hippocampus. Because hippocampal cells are serotonin inhibited, religious experience may have some relationship with this pathway—which is also involved in hallucination.

In a creative tentative discussion of "God and the Limbic System," neurologist V. S. Ramachandran asks, "Is there a 'God module' in our heads?"[22] While human beings typically seek solace in religion, Ramachandran does not think that this can fully explain flights of intense religious experience. The feeling of the presence of a Creative Presence "is so widespread in all societies all over the world that it is tempting to ask whether the propensity for such beliefs might have a biological basis."[23] On the basis of several case studies, Ramachandran states that there exist "neural structures in the temporal lobe that are specialized for religion or spirituality" and that are simply enhanced in the case of epilepsy. He states, "The one clear conclusion that emerges from all this is that there are circuits in the human brain that are involved in religious experience and these become hyperactive in some epileptics."[24] If certain brain circuits are regularly engaged with spirituality and religion, they have evolved for this purpose.

The scientific literature regarding heightened religiosity in relation to temporal-lobe epilepsy is well summarized by Jeffrey Saver and John Rabin.[25] They define the core qualities of "spiritual" experience as the noetic and the ineffable—"the sense of having touched the ultimate ground of reality and the sense of the unutterability or incommunicability of the experience."[26] They include a sense of unity, timelessness, and positive effect (especially peace and joy) as frequent additional features. They indicate that the primary substrate for this experience is the limbic system, which "integrates external stimuli with internal drives and is part of a distributed neural network that marks stimuli and events with positive or negative value."[27] They conclude:

Humanity had been called *homo religiosus*—the religious animal. Behavioral neuroscience must encompass a fully realized account of the substrates of religious experience if it is to achieve a systematic understanding of the brain basis of all human behavior. The task before neuropsychiatrists and behavioral neurologists is to fully understand brain disorders that promote, intensify, or alter religious experience—unique clues to the neural basis of the spiritual nature of humanity.[28]

In other words, by understanding the neurological correlates of religious experience we can begin to understand a unique human propensity that exists at different levels of magnitude in individual persons. In the context of nonreductive physicalism, such study does not explain religious experience away as a mere neurological event; instead, it suggests how it is that the Creative Presence can touch humanity through its highest capacity, which is latent even if unexpressed in some persons.

Fear and Security

If the existentialist theologians are right, some of the biology of spirituality may be rooted in the experience of fear and anxiety. Joseph LeDoux argues persuasively that the amygdala, two nubbins of neural tissue in the limbic system (the archaic part of the brain underlying the neocortex), long recognized as an emotional center, is the center of the "Wheel of Fear." Nerves running from the amygdala carry messages affecting heart rate, blood pressure, sweating, and other autonomic physical functions. Other nerves from the amygdala lead upwards into the cortex and areas controlling the release of stress hormones. Sensory input travels to the amygdala via the sensory thalamus. LeDoux writes:

Imagine walking in the woods. A crackling sound occurs. It goes straight to the amygdala through the thalamic pathway. The sound also goes from the thalamus to the cortex, which recognizes the sound to be a dry twig that snapped under the weight of your boot, or that of a rattlesnake shaking its tail. But by the time the cortex has figured this out, the amygdala is already starting to defend against snakes. The information received from the thalamus is unfiltered and biased toward evoking responses. The cortex's job is to prevent the inappropriate response rather than to produce the appropriate one.[29]

Given that religious experience is generally associated with a sense of security in an otherwise rather insecure existence, it can be surmised that it in part acts to relieve fear. If so, one would expect such experience to have a positive mental health impact (see chapter 3), since so much mental illness is related to fear (e.g., panic attacks, phobias, posttraumatic stress disorder, and paranoia). Security, harmoniousness, and love are all typically reported aspects of religious experience.

I do not wish to overstate the data on neuroscience and religious experience. Science is a very long way from clarity in this field of study. Clearly, however, the perennial and ineradicable aspects of religion in human experience suggest that the study of neurological correlates is worthwhile and may result in a much clearer understanding of human nature. The neuroscience of *Homo religiosus* is nascent but suggestive. Yet a number of coherent studies begin to clarify the involvement of specific brain regions in various religious experiences.[30] These studies, however, generally concern reproducible practices such as meditation, which can be studied in a controlled environment where physiological responses are measurable. Spontaneous mystical experiences or sudden religious conversions do not easily lend themselves to study. But more is being learned about these experiences, and what we know already suggests that, as Dietrich Bonhoeffer put it, there is a God-shaped space in the human soul.

But we need to be careful about the use of this term *soul*. Does spiritual and religious experience require a nonmaterial soulishness? No, although the possibility of some nonmaterial aspect of the self remains as a matter of faith. Neurological mapping of spiritual and religious experiences in no way diminishes their significance or validity, even though these are physiological rather than nonmaterial domains. Nor does such mapping suggest in any way that there is not a Creative Presence in the universe from which all ultimate meaning derives. Should people in faith traditions embrace such physiological studies? In my view, such studies begin to help us understand the persistent quality of spirituality and religion and are therefore of considerable public significance.

Neurology and the "Soul"

Critics of the argument that human beings are by nature spiritual and religious creatures wrongly believe that discoveries of neurological correlates undermine religious worldviews. They correctly point to the fact that the neurosciences have already explained many or all the capacities once attributed to the nonmaterial soul—a fact that many theologians comfortably accept.[31] They are also correct in pointing out that world religions have recognized a nonmaterial soul as the point of contact between the human being and a Creative Presence, although this is actually not as uniform as they assert. Judaism, for example, does not assert a nonmaterial soul; yet it is a tradition of prayer and of mystical union with God. Where the critics are in error is in arguing that spirituality and religion depend on the existence of some nonmaterial "soul," when in fact these capacities can emerge in a purely neurological substrate over the course of human evolution. It is regrettable that so many people think that once the idea of a nonmaterial soul goes, spirituality and religion must be deemed passé; in fact a non-material God should be able to interact with a human creature through its neural substrate. I assert this without any hesitancy, although I am by no means myself convinced that a non-material soul might not exist at some level of being.

The brain, though, is an estimated three pounds of soft material stuff that is a web of communicating cells as complex and mystifying as the universe is to the astronomer. From a scientific perspective, there is no empirical basis from which to posit a nonmaterial "spiritual" substrate to explain the religious propensity. *Homo religiosus* may be revalorized scientifically in response to its detractors if a capacity to sense a Creative Presence can be studied as an aspect of human neurological evolution, along the same lines as capacities for speech, abstract thinking, and vision. Although science in this area is in its infancy, *Homo religiosus* may ultimately be shown to have a brain substrate or correlate that enables (in contrast to causes) awareness of a Creative Presence.

Unless this substrate of human religiousness can be clarified scientifically, scientists such as Francis Crick, among others, can continue to assert that neuroscience has relegated religion to the wastebasket of the archaic. "Most religions," he writes, "hold that some kind of spirit exists that persists after one's bodily death and, to some degree, embodies the essence of that human being."[32] Further, "a modern neurobiologist sees no need for the religious concept of a soul to explain the behavior of humans and other animals."[33] With this explosion of the myth, moreover, educated persons are bound to fall into the categories of "atheists, agnostics, humanists, or just lapsed believers" who deny "the major claims of the traditional religions."[34] Crick holds that the explanation of our mental capacities in terms of nerve cells and neurochemistry has made religion absurd. But to repeat an earlier point, in my view there is no reason why the human perception of a Creative Presence has to rest upon an immaterial substrate.

Theists who insist on the necessity of an immaterial soul play into Crick's hands. Crick dismisses, for example, Sir John C. Eccles, a Nobel laureate in neuroscience, who wrote:

> Since materialist solutions fail to account for our experienced uniqueness, I am constrained to attribute the uniqueness of the Self or Soul to a supernatural spiritual creation. To give the explanation in theological terms: each Soul is a new Divine creation which is implanted into the growing foetus at some time between conception and birth.[35]

Assertions such as that of Eccles, however, are the result of a Platonic theory of "substance" dualism, often positing a natural (inferior, visible) body and a supernatural (superior, invisible) soul. Eccles thus echoes a time-honored dualism that is increasingly untenable in the light of the neurosciences; it is a form of "vitalism" that suggests some entity or substance added to the biological in order to constitute the person. Eccles may be correct, but there is no scientific argument for his view. When theologians such as Keith Ward and Richard Swinburne argue for the nonmaterial soul on scientific grounds, they are really providing an apologetic for their commitment to substance dualism, rather than developing a significant scientific case.[36] They may be correct, but their position is clearly doctrinal rather than empirical.

Purely for the sake of argument—I do not personally reject the idea of a nonmaterial soul—let us take the position of nonreductive physicalism, which means that while human beings do not possess a nonmaterial soul, they do possess the capacity for relationship with a Creative Presence that is "supervenient" on biological events, not caused by them. Nonreductive physicalism accepts ontological reduction—the idea that human beings are composed of the molecular stuff of reality and possess nothing nonmaterial; however, it rejects causal reductionism, the thesis that the whole is nothing more than the sum of its parts and is fully explicable in terms of molecular activity. Nonreductive physicalism by no means suggests that scientists can logically discard the possibility of a Creative Presence and its relationship with human beings; on the contrary, concepts of a Creative Presence and correlative human perception must now be considered with scientific seriousness.

"Phase Change" Emergence and Nonreductive Physicalism

Nonreductive physicalism is one form of "monism," the view in metaphysics and ontology that stresses the oneness of reality in its essential aspects. A physicalist monism postulates that this reality is substantive (rather than the mere projection of mind) and that there is nothing in human nature beyond what is presented—that is, that reality is undivided.. The nonreductive form of physicalism, which rejects the notion of separate or divisible soul and body, still asserts the human capacity for a relationship with a Creative Presence who acts upon the human in a manner that is consistent with freedom. (Nonreductive physicalism asserts free will; physical-neurological events do not determine mental ones.)

Nonreductive physicalism understands the human as "a physical organism whose complex functioning, both in society and in relation to God, gives rise to 'higher' human capacities such as emotion, morality, and spirituality."[37] This view, then, does not include an immortal, immaterial soul, though neither does it falsify this possibility. As Etienne Gilson wrote in his 1931–32 Gifford Lectures, the idea of an immortal soul is not as essential to Christianity as might be assumed, although it is an idea that does hold sway in the tradition:

> It would probably surprise a good many modern Christians to learn that in certain of the earliest Fathers the belief in the immortality of the soul is vague almost to non-existence. This, nevertheless, is a fact, and a fact to be noted, because it casts so strong a light on the point on which Christian anthropology turns and on the course of its historical development. A Christianity without the immortality of the soul is not, in the long run, absolutely inconceivable, and the proof of it is that it has been conceived. What really would be absolutely inconceivable would be a Christianity without the resurrection of the Man.[38]

Gilson, the twentieth century's leading interpreter of medieval theology—and of the thought of Thomas Aquinas in particular—asserts the immortality of the soul, but with the recognition that Christianity has entertained physicalist views of human nature without anxiety. He does not consider the nonmaterial soul to be a requirement of Christian belief. Aquinas, who was influenced by Aristotle, resisted much of Platonic dualism; he emphasized the unity of the human nature and associated "soul" with "form."

Thus the history of Christian thought on the nature of the human being is quite complex and varied. Ignorance of this variation, however, has resulted in the uninformed pitting of the monistic, physicalist, and naturalist traditions against religion (supernature) in general and Christianity in particular. The utilitarian philosopher Jeremy Bentham (d. 1832), for example, denied the existence of an immortal soul and considered this to be an argument for atheism. Yet theism is perfectly compatible with a nonreductive physicalism that allows a neurological grounding for all human experience, while providing a probable account of a Creative Presence's actions upon the human being.

Nonreductive physicalism is a position first described by the philosopher Roy Wood Sellars. His view was that no new "metaphysical" ingredients, such as a nonmaterial soul, are necessary to describe "higher" human capacities.[39] The basic "stuff" of the physical world can reach higher levels of organization so that genuinely new and real capacities emerge. Sellers examined the organization of physical substrate at the inorganic, organic, mental (or conscious), social, ethical, and religious-spiritual levels.[40] "We ask, therefore, could it be that the same material 'stuff'—brains of animals as well as humans—due to changes in structural complexity, at some point undergo something analogous to a 'phase change' so that new properties of mind, consciousness, and a capacity for spiritual awareness emerge in humans"?[41] Malcolm Jeeves rejects the dualism of Eccles, but he just as surely rejects what he calls the "nothing buttery" of Crick (i.e., that religious experience is "nothing but" the action of the brain).[42] Human awareness of the Supreme Being requires a neural substrate at its sufficiently developed organizational level, coupled with the active presence of that Supreme Being. Human religiosity and dignity are still composed of a real relationship with the Supreme Being.

Similarly, neuroscientist Warren S. Brown writes of "emergenesis" as a kind of neurological "phase change." An emergent property "is a unique mode of functioning that becomes possible on the basis of both a significant increase in the capacity of some number of lower-level abilities and the interaction among these capacities."[43] The emergent property cannot be fully understood by scrutiny of the lower capacities, and the property may have a "downward causative influence" on those lower capacities.[44] Thus, according to nonreductive physicalism, religious experience can be grounded in a new organizational development of the human brain and may be to some extent more pronounced in certain genotypes.[45]

Of course, the whole problem here for the substance dualist is that he or she does not see how we can be "getting more out of less." How, the dualist will argue, can a Creative Presence, who is by definition not a physical entity (not material and not bound by the space-time-cause-effect continuum) have communion with a purely physical entity? The next section tries to explain this notion of emergence more fully.

Religion, "Phase Change," and Evolutionary Process

A religious explosion took place in human neurological organization between 30,000 and 60,000 years ago in our species. *Homo sapiens sapiens* was first seen 100,000 years ago sharing the scene with both the Neanderthals and archaic *Homo sapiens*. Steven Mithen describes the evolution of language, technical intelligence, social intelligence, and natural history intelligence as a "whole series of cultural sparks that occur at slightly different times in different parts of the world between 60,000 and 30,000 years ago."[46] Suddenly, for example, we see the production of remarkably complex and beautiful ivory statuettes and cave paintings. The paintings in Chauvet Cave (30,000 B.C.E.) are splendid: "Although this is the very first art known to humankind, there is nothing primitive about it."[47] Mithen sees nothing gradual about this development, as he compares the beauty of cave art to the great works of the Renaissance. (The impressive horses, engraved owl, and rhinoceri on the walls of the Grotte Chauvet were created 32,000 years ago.[48]) Mithen attributes this human capacity to "new connections between the domains of technical, social and natural history intelligence."[49] Previously compartmentalized capacities in the brain could now interact, making possible a new magnitude of integrative creativity. At this same time, we see the emergence of religion, as evidenced by rituals that were intended to harness higher powers to bring about change in the natural world. Ritual activities, including religious burials concerned with afterlife, are evident in the anthropological record.[50] Mithen refers to a "big bang" in the history of human religious, artistic, and technical capacities due to a new fluidity of consciousness. Such an interpretation of the emergence of spiritual experience is consistent with nonreductive physicalism and with the current picture of human evolution.

This explosion in human capacities is the dawning of a new morning in the evolution of life on earth. It is the dewy hour of sunrise in the springtime of consciousness. For the theist who, against the background of the anthropic principle, surmises some divine action mysteriously underlying the emergence of a creature who can now feel the presence of a Creative Presence, this is all a story of Cosmic Process. The sources of this new morning are found in the deepest foundations of the universe, in the far-off beginnings of the cosmos. The universe was "set up" to give rise to a creature whose evolution would now be in increments of neurological capacity and, eventually, of spirituality and culture. The highest goal of the Creative Presence was to establish background conditions in the universe that would eventually allow for the neurological capacities of the one creature with whose life that Presence might have relationship.

Religious sentiment must be added to the differentiation of the human creature through the emergence of language, art, and technique. This sentiment would go on to shape history, art, and literature. Along with the first stammerings of speech and the dawning ethical discrimination between right and wrong came the earliest dim recognition of a presence in the universe greater than our own, in harmony with which rests our fuller well-being. This religious capacity, like speech, is hard-wired into the neurological substrate. It would be more fully realized over the course of civilization at times such as Karl Jaspers's "axial period," in the fifth century B.C.E., when Malachi, Buddha, Socrates, and Zoroaster, among others, affected their cultures. While it may be inhibited in certain periods, it is powerful enough to reassert itself.

Any student of human evolution knows that it wastes no time in adapting a creature successfully to its environment. The eye evolves to better see the world around it, the ear to better perceive the sounds. Does it not make sense, then, to suggest that the religious capacity evolved in response to something objective, something that really exists? After two centuries of denial of a Creative Presence by cadres of intellectuals, the presence of religious sentiment remains as dominant as ever among people of all walks of life across all cultures. The positivist philosophy of Comte and Freud—that religion would fade in the twentieth century to nothing—has been entirely refuted. Is this not the best argument for spirituality and religion as an essential and, therefore, ineradicable feature of the truly human?

One of the twentieth century's most influential religious thinkers, Rudolph Otto, used the word *numen* to describe the fundamental objective grounding of the experience of the holy.[51] The numinous experience is a feeling of blank wonder, absolute astonishment, and stupor before a mysterious "wholly other." The experience, which is overpowering and transforming, includes elements of awe and fear as well as fascination. It is an experience that is qualitatively different from all those aroused by natural sense data, such as music. Like such natural sense experiences, however, it does have an objective referent and engages what Otto describes as a faculty of divination—or what I would refer to as a neurological correlate. This numinous knowledge is evoked by a hidden but real presence of a being greater than our own that is incommensurate with ordinary realities; because it involves knowledge of an object, it is objective rather than subjective, even if it contains subjective interpretive elements.

According to Otto, the religious faculty is ubiquitously latent. It is developed to its maximum in the prophetic figures who convey the nature of their experience to others in such deeply impassioned ways that one concludes that something was indeed experienced. The nature of the experience itself provides certainty of an objectively veridical feeling. For most of us, religious experience of the "wholly other" is less intense and is mediated through symbols, rituals, and worship.

Other phenomenologists of religion, such as John Baillie, would add to Otto's thought the notion that the "wholly other" is also the *summum bonum* or source of true human well-being, a topic pursued in the next chapter.[52] While awe and shuddering are part of religious experience, John Oman would add that this rather intimidating emphasis must be balanced with creativity, peace, and joy.[53] In a word, Oman replaced "awe" with "wow." Mircea Eliade would focus on the symbolic and mythological representation of the experience of the "wholly other."[54] Consistent throughout this literature is a descriptive effort that discerns certitude, definiteness, and objectivity in spiritual and religious experience.

Human Dignity and Nonreductive Physicalism

What does the rise of neuroscientific physicalism, in which "higher capacities" such as the capacity to relate to a Creative Presence are explained in terms of neurological correlates, mean to religious conceptions of human dignity? Reductive physicalism, of course, is nothing but the modern materialism that permits the easy destruction of human lives, which lack any higher spiritual features conferring inviolability. The atheistic materialism of Marxist-Leninism, for example, displayed little regard for human life; secular existentialism also counts life rather cheaply. Nonreductive physicalism, however, contrasts sharply with the reductive variety, for it is neither atheistic nor undermining of our relationship with a Creative Presence.

I do not, however, think that the sanctity of human life is grounded in the notion of the immaterial soul; rather, it is grounded in the capacity (or potential) of the human being to be in a relationship with a Creative Presence. The distinction between brain causation and brain correlation continues to be important in this regard. Unfortunately, even neuroscientists sometimes confuse the two. The fact that the neurological correlate(s) of religious experience can be intelligently discussed and researched does not mean that such experiences are caused by the brain—even if, in some abnormal conditions, the relevant parts of the brain are activated in ways that mimic authentic religious experience that involves the Creative Presence.

The problem of confusing cause with correlate has been highlighted by psychologists, who view the cause of certain behaviors (e.g., attention deficit hyperactivity disorder [ADHD]) to be environmental and relational, as neuroscientists point out areas of the brain and brain transmitters that are involved. Richard J. Degrandpre, for example, writes of ADHD and many other conditions that "as technological advances have offered a closer look at the brain's connection to human thought and action, they have also enabled biological psychiatrists and neuroscientists to promote a dangerous institutional bias toward neurological reductionism."[55] It is absurd to assume that any simply physiological correlate of an experience or behavior is good evidence of a cause.

Human dignity is, I have stated, grounded in our capacity for a relationship with a Creative Presence, even if that capacity is inhibited; by pointing to potential brain correlates, nonreductive physicalism enhances the credibility and significance of this relationship for those who find substance dualism to be scientifically troubling. Substance dualism, however, cannot be disproven. Those such as Eccles, who wish to see a hint of something other than the neuronal substrate as constitutive of the soul, may someday be proven right. If human dignity rests on a point of connection with the Creative Presence, however, nonreductive physicalism suffices.

The dualism that I most associate here with adverse moral consequences can plausibly be derived from Plato and Descartes, but not from Aristotle and Aquinas. The dualism of Plato is not that of Descartes; it is also certainly not that of Aristotle, Thomas Aquinas, and the scholastic tradition, for which the soul is the substantial form of the body rather than a separate entity or substance.

Is substance dualism the cause of patriarchy, slavery, and the debasement of the body? Or is it the other way around? My claim is not for a clearly causal relationship between substance dualism and these regrettable realities—for surely history is more complex in the etiology of wrongfulness. I only assert a certain affinity between ideas and social practices.

Whether or not substance dualism has been a seedbed of oppression, Christian ethics has been undermined in some instances by the use of the analogy of dualism and the dualistic account of human nature to distinguish between a superior soul and an inferior human body and between superior (male, free) beings and inferior (female, slave) human beings. Substance dualism has served as an ideological support for the exclusionary inclination ("might makes right") to place categories of human beings outside of ordinary restraints on wanton infliction of harm and coercion.

A major justification for slavery emerged from a substance-dualistic conception of the human person. Plato, for example, likened the body to the slave of the soul. The relationship of body and soul informed a political apologetic for slavery.[56] The master-slave relationship was couched in a cosmology perceived as a similar dualism (intelligent divine primary cause and irrational mechanical cause). Thus, slavery was supported by an appeal to natural law—that is, because the soul has total dominion over the body, the master should have total dominion over the slave.[57] Despite his departure from Plato's substance dualism, Aristotle still followed Plato in rationalizing slavery by showing its consistency with the order of being.

A purported benefit of dualism has been the argument that the presence of a soul confers equal moral worth on all humans. Radical dualism (the soul or mind is separable from the body, and the person is identified with the former) purportedly confers a protective canopy over those imperiled and vulnerable people at the very margins of human mental capacity. The most severe cases of retardation or advanced irreversible progressive dementia only hinder the expression of the invisible soul, which in fact still exists in all its eternal value under the veneer of confusion. Therefore (so the argument would go), caregivers need never think that their loved one is no longer present, that they have before them only a "shell," "husk," or "half-empty" glass. Indeed, the glass is still full because the soul is still there, even if camouflaged by neurological devastation. Such lives are worthy of all the moral consideration and standing that we would ordinarily bestow upon those of us who are more neurologically intact.

Wolf Wolfensberger, one of the best known advocates for people with retardation, describes the threat of "deathmaking" through the denial of life-saving treatment or euthanasia. He contends that this threat builds on "modernistic values" that include various elements, the most prominent being materialism: "The first element of modernism is a materialistic worldview which denies the existence (or at least the relevance) of any immaterial, spiritual dimensions to reality and life, and instead embraces a materialistic, mechanistic, reductionistic way of relating to reality, including human beings."[58] This materialism "views the human as a mere body, without a soul, and certainly not made in the image and likeness of God. Therefore, there resides no absolute transcendent value in the individual human."[59] One might disagree with such a statement for its radical dualism but nevertheless appreciate the inclusion of the most imperiled among us under the protection of the principle of nonmaleficence.

The nineteenth-century historian W. E. H. Lecky argued that the early Christian tradition, with its Platonic dualistic image of the self, deepened the sense of the sanctity of human life—that is, every self has an invisible soul that is the seat of equality. Lecky's *History of European Morals* describes the discountenancing of infanticide by the Christian Church, which thereby broke decisively with the conventional morality of the Roman Empire. Lecky juxtaposed the Christian ethics of *agape* (universal love, especially concerned with the vulnerable) with the ethics of Rome in these pointed terms:

> Whatever mistakes may have been made, the entire movement I have traced displays an anxiety not only for the life, but also for the moral well-being, of the castaways of society, such as the most humane nations of antiquity had never reached. This minute and scrupulous care for human life and human virtue in the humblest forms, in the slave, the gladiator, the savage, or the infant, was indeed wholly foreign to the genius of Paganism. It was produced by the Christian doctrine of the *inestimable value of each immortal soul* [italics mine].[60]

From the notion of people as immortal and sacred beings "grew up the eminently Christian idea of the sanctity of all human life."[61] Although undeveloped and in this sense less significant than adult life, infant life nevertheless possessed a fearful significance because the soul was destined for hell unless saved by baptism. Those with deranged or demented minds also had a sanctity equal to that of persons whose capacities were spared, for they were still ensouled.

But should we uncritically accept Lecky's statement that this "scrupulous care for human life" was the result of "the inestimable value of each immortal soul"? Despite a dualistic view of the self, infanticide was widely accepted in Plato's Athens and was specifically defended as a method of population control in his *Republic*. More likely, this "scrupulous care" results from the example of *agape* or "unlimited love" manifest in Christ.

Richard Tarnas writes of Western ethics as bringing about "a vital concern for every human soul, no matter what level of intelligence or culture was brought to the spiritual enterprise, and without regard to physical strength or beauty or social status."[62] This is a fair summarization with which nonreductive physicalism can accord; it allows for the existence of the "soul" in the sense of a human relationship with a Creative Presence. The "concern" emerges from the demonstration of divine love, rather than from a particular view of the "soul."

Religious Experience as Participation in Unlimited Love

Nonreductive physicalists Nancey Murphy and George Ellis see echoes of unlimited love in nature and in human nature but argue that these echoes await resonance with more expansive chords from God. Religious experience is essential in the expansive process:

> Thus, we will assume that there must be a channel through which God can act in a noninterventionist manner, in order

to make available visions of ultimate reality to persons open to them—allowing the nature of that transcendent reality to make itself known, making available to us new patterns of understanding, and providing encouragement and strength to follow these visions.[63]

Attuned to the Quaker tradition of an "inner light," these authors suggest a possible brain correlate "at the quantum level within the human nervous system."[64]

Authentic religious experience, argued William James, is anything but self-preoccupying. The practical fruit of such experience must be heightened altruism. The "ripe fruits of religion" are universally understood in terms of saintliness, which includes these features: a sense of the existence of an Ideal Power, a self-surrender to its control, a sense of elation and freedom, and "a shifting of the emotional centre toward loving and harmonious affections, towards 'yes, yes,' and away from 'no,' where the claims of the non-ego are concerned."[65] Religious experience in relation to charity is defined thus: "The shifting of the emotional centre brings, secondly, increased charity, tenderness, for fellow-creatures. The ordinary motives to antipathy, *which usually set such close bounds to tenderness among human beings,* are inhibited. The saint loves his enemies, and treats loathsome beggars as his brothers [italics mine]."[66] Further, "[b]rotherly love would follow logically from the assurance of God's friendly presence, the notion of our brotherhood as men being an immediate inference from that of God's fatherhood of us all."[67] The "altruistic impulses" become more marked.[68] Solicitude and universal goodwill abound.

James has captured an essential feature of religious experience. Unfortunately, this "phase change," which constitutes a truly moral life, can be violated by insular tendencies. Much conflict in the world is the result of exclusive in-group loyalties that are sometimes exacerbated by religious arrogance. Humility is an important virtue with regard to truth claims about the precise nature of ultimate reality.[69]

Evolutionary Biology

The fact that the "phase change" of altruism toward radical inclusivity is hampered by insular tendencies should come as no surprise. Many evolutionary biologists tell us that we are morally limited: we will behave altruistically to protect close relatives because they carry our same genes; we will exchange favors within a group in order to enhance our survival and that of kin; we will cooperate with others in pursuing a difficult goal if this is in our self-interest.[70] Matt Ridley, a commentator on evolutionary biology, is frankly pessimistic about human beings' achieving universal altruism. He sees much good in reciprocal altruism but also sees that "universal benevolence is impossibly Utopian."[71] Cooperation enhances inclusive genetic success, and cooperators seek out cooperators: "Think about it: reciprocity hangs, like a sword of Damocles, over every human head."[72] The evolutionary origins incline us to a mere reciprocal altruism. Our tribalism is "the consequence of our evolutionary heritage as coalition-building, troop-living apes."[73]

Robert Wright, whose assessment of evolutionary biology and psychology holds human nature to be less amenable to reason's dictates, sees a role for religion:

Altruism, compassion, empathy, love, conscience, the sense of justice—all of these things, the things that hold society together, the things that allow our species to think so highly of itself, can now confidently be said to have a firm genetic basis. That's the good news. The bad news is that, although these things are in some ways blessings for humanity as a whole, they didn't evolve for the "good of the species" and aren't reliably employed to that end. Quite the contrary: it is now clearer than ever how (and precisely why) the moral sentiments are used with brutal flexibility, switched on and off in keeping with self-interest; and how naturally oblivious we often are to this switching.[74]

The moral sentiments exist within human coalitions that compete for status and therefore have both positive and negative implications. In the process, we take credit even if undeserved, engage in self-inflation, and deflate the reputation of others with conviction, even though the truth has been twisted. Information is manipulated to one's advantage, and credibility grows with prestige.

Wright argues that religion and spirituality are about "the defiance of human nature in some measure."[75] He believes that our moral sentiments are often tools of survival applied selectively to our advantage; religion wishes to save the sentiments but demolish the status seeking and tactical alliances that breed inhumanity. It is not "Do unto others as they have done unto you," but "Love thy neighbor."

James Q. Wilson draws on evolutionary biology when asserting that "our moral sense" emerged and operates "in small groups more than in large ones, to say nothing of embracing mankind as a whole."[76] Our capacity for sympathy is forged in the mother-child relationship, Wilson contends, and is "expanded by the enlarged relationships of families and peers."[77] All this is good and necessary. However,

Because our moral senses are at origin parochial and easily blunted by even trivial differences between what we think of as familiar and what we define as strange, it is not hard to explain why there is so much misery in the world and thus easy to understand why so many people deny the existence of a moral sense at all. How can there be a moral sense if everywhere we find cruelty and combat, sometimes on a monstrous scale?[78]

We are too easily ethnic and genocidal. Sympathy is limited in range and always the rival of anger, aggression, and greed. Human altruism is sometimes quite inclusive, as in the case of adoption or of the lone bystander who helps an endangered person. Sometimes "sentiment alone, unsupported by utility," rises to action.[79] Still, the moral sense, which is essentially the capacity for sympathy, is "not a strong beacon of light," but "a small candle flame."[80]

Perhaps natural human altruism is not quite as narrowly reciprocal as the evolutionary biologists indicate. A minority view among the scientists themselves allows for a freeing of the capacity for sympathy from the confines of genetic interests. Elliot Sober and David Sloan Wilson, for example, argue that altruism, which "attributes to people ultimate desires concerning the welfare of individuals other than themselves,"[81] is a powerful presence in human motivation, due in large part to group selection, the influence of culture, and the plasticity of human capacities. Even if Sober and Wilson are correct, their thesis still does not solve the problem of in-group versus out-group conflict.

Suffice it to say that human creatures are not inclined to universal altruism simply by our biological nature.[82] We are not biased in this direction by evolution, even though the underlying capacities for empathy and reflection on past actions are neurologically given. A "phase change" is required to achieve universal love. We have at times seen those among us who seem to have made this change with the help, they claim, of the transforming presence of a Creative Presence.

How do we transcend the deeply biological insularity that limits our altruism to kin, reciprocators, or the in-group? Moral philosophers have prescribed their theories of universal respect, dignity, and regard. But reason is a limited spur to action, incapable of the holistic "phase change" that must occur at the affective level.

Universal care must be activated by something more than theories, although theories can be interesting. Utilitarianism, of course, is not overly expansionist; in its pure form it is willing to sacrifice 49 percent of the people for the so-called happiness of the 51 percent. Arch-utilitarian Peter Singer is naive about the purity and power of reason but is correct in asserting that "our present ethical systems have their roots in the altruistic behavior of our early human and pre-human ancestors."[83] Agreeing with the evolutionary biologists that the gene is the ultimate unit of evolution, Singer writes:

> Evolution will favor, other things being equal, behavior which improves the prospects of my children surviving and reproducing. Thus the first and most obvious way in which evolution can produce altruism is the concern of parents for their children. This is so widespread and natural a form of altruism that we do not usually think of it as altruism at all.[84]

Genes that lead parents to care for children are more likely to survive than ones that don't. Because genes can also survive in kin, kin altruism extends beyond the parental-child axis to a larger circle. Reciprocal altruism would have obvious advantages for survival, but it is shaped by a "tit for tat" quality that kin altruism does not have. It does likely lead to "a more general tendency for altruistic behavior toward other members of a group."[85] Concern for reciprocity within a group would lead to some hostility toward outsiders, which is "a very common phenomenon in social animals."[86] Singer argues that ethics is the superimposition of reason on otherwise narrow helping impulses. It is ethical reason that moves us beyond the tensions and conflicts between groups to a universal viewpoint. Reason shows us that outsiders share our own capacities and interests and are, therefore, not beyond the protective umbrella of non-maleficence.

Singer's appreciation for the roots of ethics in human nature is impressive, but his optimism concerning reason is not substantiated by the facts of human history; reason is rarely, if ever, divorced from self-interest and status seeking. Ethical theories can intellectualize about universalism, but emotion (which is rooted in the limbic system) is needed to affect will: what is simply understood is not simply achieved. This gap between the sense of "ought" and our natural propensities gives rise to the "symbolism of evil." Even the greatest of philosophers, Socrates, did not depend on reason alone—he received a mission from the Oracle at Delphi. In the words of Henri Bergson, "All the great mystics declare that they have the impression of a current passing from their soul to God, and flowing back again from God to mankind."[87] The insular tendencies of natural altruistic propensities directed to the near and dear, especially kin, must be transcended. The extensive must absorb the narrow, and this hinges on something more than pure reason. The culmination of religious experience is energetic active love implemented in effective ways. In Bergson's words, "Through God, in the strength of God, he loves all mankind with a divine love. This is not the fraternity enjoined on us by the philosophers in the name of reason, on the principle that all men share by birth in one rational essence."[88] The noble ideal of respect based on shared rational agency deserves some consideration, but this ideal is not the spur to willed action.

Arguably, moral "emergenesis" or "phase change" does not occur without a power as deeply transforming as religious experience. Religious experience cannot be merely the source of inner peace, joy, and security. *Homo religiosus* must also be a being of universal other-regarding sentiments. Natural other-regarding human sentiments (solicitude, sympathy, compassion) that shape acts of loving kindness toward kin (family) and reciprocators (friends) can expand to change a world of strangers into a world of neighbors. Even the major moral philosophers were interpreting the inclusivity of moral life bequeathed from religion in secular terms. John Stuart Mill quoted the New Testament command to love thy neighbor, and Kant's idea of respect emerged from his German Lutheran pietist background. In contrast to Kant, however, Mill was not a theist.

I believe that ultimately this universal solicitude (affective and cognitive) is sustained by the conviction that a caring Creative Presence exists at the center of the universe; this is a belief rooted historically in the great world religions and is a condition for their success. The ideal of universal love encompasses the better aspects of all spiritual and religious traditions. Mother Teresa and Gandhi are cherished because they seem to have gotten beyond narrow forms of altruism that are both wonderful in their promise and pernicious in their out-group aggression. (It should be noted that, according to E. O. Wilson, Mother Teresa and other religious altruists are self-interested, pursuing personal salvation and the security of an established in-group that congeals identity and purpose in life: "There lies the fountainhead of religious altruism."[89])

There is a plasticity and freedom in the expression of empathy and in acts of kindness that must not be denied. But the exaltation of altruism directed toward the stranger who is considered neighbor occurs in the matrix of religious experience and religious cultures. *Homo religiosus* looks toward divinity as an essential step toward existential security and discovers that the perception of the divine carries with it a blessed passion to care for all humanity. Religious experience, then, is essential to peace both within the individual and within the world.

Envoi: Human Evolution and the Objectivity
of a Creative Presence

Can it be absolutely proven that the human person is indeed *Homo religiosus?* Even E. O. Wilson, whose interpretation of religion is highly reductive and suspicious of all saintliness as disguising the pursuit of reputation gain, writes as follows: "The predisposition to religious belief is the most complex and powerful force in the human mind and in all probability an ineradicable part of human nature."[90]

Rabbi Michael Lerner, editor of *Tikkun,* calls "for a 'politics in the image of God,' an attempt to reconstruct the world in a way that takes seriously the uniqueness and preciousness of every human being and our connection to a higher ethical and spiritual purpose that gives meaning to our lives."[91] Or, as the Czech poet-president Vaclav Havel argues, the current crises in our world are "directly related to the spiritual condition of modern civilization. This condition is characterized by loss: the loss of metaphysical certainties, of an experience of the transcendental, of any superpersonal moral authority, and of any kind of higher horizon."[92] University of Michigan social scientist Ronald Inglehart concludes from value surveys across the Western world that we are seeing the beginnings of a decline in materialist values and a heightened interest in religiosity.[93] Gallup reports that 96 percent of Americans believe in "God, or a universal spirit" and that 84 percent think this Supreme Being is accessible through prayer.[94] Even the most casual perusal of best-seller lists, magazine covers, and other aspects of popular culture indicates that religiosity is anything but obsolete.[95]

I have argued that *Homo religiosus* begins with an "emergenesis" from the flux of neurological evolution, thereby parting company with even its most proximate nonhuman relations by virtue of a sense of imminent Presence. The anthropology and history of religions fully document a perennial craving to relate to and even to know a Creative Presence. In some individuals and periods, this craving may be either relatively pronounced or embryonic. When the capacity of *Homo religiosus* is awakened, there is an awareness of greater than "natural" moral demand; our Western Enlightenment theories of ethics place an emphasis on universal inclusivity that is bequeathed to them from the spirituality and religion from which it arose.

A detached and impartial observer of the species can only say that we are now, and have always been, *Homo religiosus,* and that progress in the extension of moral standing to humanity universally considered has its roots in some form of spiritual self-transformation. The hard historical fact is that our species has a brain anxious to transcend the world of "ordinary" sense and "ordinary" nature to a pattern of correspondence with a Creative Presence. Augustine spoke of love for God: "For there is a joy that is not given to those who do not love you, but only to those who love you for your own sake."[96] Thomas Aquinas would continue the Augustinian emphasis on God as our ultimate "chief end."[97] If the record of human religious and spiritual activity is considered, these claims have a certain obvious validity.

It is difficult to conceive of this brain-based correlate in the absence of a Reality to which this capacity is a response. Nature does not waste its energies. Religiosity—prayer, faith, symbolic representation, sanctification—distinguishes the human from the nonhuman. Other primates do not pray. We do. Those among us with a highly developed religious sense have a particular fascination with this Reality and characteristically teach a universal loving kindness. There are many forms of religious experience: the interpretation of events within a religious framework of meaning, which requires no special experience but can nonetheless have tremendous importance; ritual worship and prayer; quasi-sensory experiences, such as dreams or visions, as well as moments of insight or inspiration, all of which might be considered revelatory; regenerative experiences that bring forgiveness, new hope, and a changed outlook; and mystical experiences that include a dramatic sense of freedom from self and ego. These sorts of experiences, all of which have the common referent of a spiritual presence greater than our own, are so widespread across cultures and times that one is tempted to assert the philosopher Swinburne's "Principle of Credulity"—that these experiences point toward a Reality (in the absence of special considerations). In other words, if it seems to the experiencing subject that a Supreme Being is present, it probably is.[98] We assume, after all, that a cat evolves whiskers to perceive objective realities; the same can be said of the capacity for religious perception. The physicist-philosopher-theologian Willem B. Drees, however, rightly warns against our being "too generous" in thinking that any experience of God is veridical.[99] Drees points out that a higher degree of skepticism is required in the realm of religious experiences, where the object cannot be corroborated in the same sense as a table or a chair.

Although I share Drees's cautions, I do not wish to psychologize the religious dimension of human experience. Given the usual connection between selectively evolved capacity and the objective environment in which that evolution takes place, the objectivity of a Creative Presence as the *summum bonum* is remarkably plausible.

The idea that the human being is by nature inclined toward a Creative Presence is of course an essential feature of the classical natural law tradition associated most powerfully with the tradition of Thomas Aquinas. If the reader finds some of the evidence thus far presented in support of *Homo religiosus* to be compelling or even plausible, then it is necessary to take an additional step into the natural law tradition. In the next chapter, I attempt to embellish that tradition with a scientific perspective. If the human being really is spiritual and religious by nature, this fact has important implications in support of freedom of religious expression in both private and public.

CHAPTER THREE

Natural Law and Natural Rights

The plausibility of a natural human spiritual and religious propensity suggests that the human being may be as much *Homo religiosus* as *Homo ludens* or *Homo sapiens*. There are, of course, those who feel for brief or protracted periods that they are alone in the universe, and for whom there is no "Big Picture" to provide meaning to existence. Such individuals may be highly compassionate and creative, and they too have their various ultimate concerns and deep human purposes that make life worthwhile. But their particular sensibilities should not obscure the larger spiritual and religious narrative of human experience.

I maintain that any flourishing public world must take the religious inclination seriously and allow its expression, for the spiritually censored citizen will experience a bifurcation of consciousness and a sense of diminishment. A genuinely liberal public world is not one that pushes religious expression into the underground of privatization, as though such free expression were an obstacle to liberal democracy rather than its essential underpinning. The anthropological argument for *Homo religiosus* presses us directly to the matter of natural law (essential beneficial inclinations) and correlative natural rights.

The ancient idea of natural law identifies those human "goods" (ends, pursuits, inclinations) without which human flourishing is improperly limited. As Leo Strauss argued, classical natural law began with the ideal of a good life defined as "life in accordance with the natural order of man's being, the life that flows from a well-ordered or healthy soul."[1] "Human flourishing" is meant to render the Greek *eudaimonia* (usually translated as "happiness" but a better word would be "excellence") more accurately. Natural law makes two presuppositions: there is an ultimate end of human life (flourishing), and there is a greater-than-human lawgiver, whether that lawgiver be the providential order of the universe or God. Classically, communion with a Creative Presence has been central to the natural law notion of true flourishing, and the cosmos is understood as unfolding toward such communion as its highest purpose. The theme of this chapter, and of this essay generally, is that *we are naturally inclined toward that Creative Presence* and that *this is as important a grounding of religious freedom as are appeals to freedom or autonomy alone.*

The Morality of Natural Law

In the wake of the Second World War, the philosopher Jacques Maritain proposed that our Western faith in human rights would require a deepened foundation after the failures of the twentieth century. He argued that we require a natural law theory that clarifies some of the underlying consistent aspects of human well-being. As Maritain wrote, human beings have "intelligible necessities" or ends that derive from an "essential constitution" that can be understood and freely pursued. The natural moral law is nothing more or less than the pursuit of the essential goods necessary for human nature to flourish.[2] This attunement of the self with the ends demanded by universal human nature is a free act and, therefore, an ethical one. By analogy, a musical instrument such as a piano has as its end the production of tuned sounds, no matter what particular brand or form of piano it is. All human beings have a right to flourish humanly; from this right, various obligations arise.

Theories of natural law include the good of life itself. Every human being has basic needs for the sustaining of life itself; acts or conditions that imperil this need, such as killing or lack of access to basic health care, are immoral. Every human being has a need to be loved from infancy by parents who convey to the child his or her value and beauty through devotion of their time, attention, and tenderness. Jean Vanier is the founder of l'Arche, an international network of communities to care for persons with intellectual disabilities. He points out that caring for such persons requires one to begin by revealing to the individual his or her value and worth.[3] Every human being, especially in his or her childhood development, has a need for play, friends, and education. Every human being has a need to be creative in whatever manner his or her physical, emotional, intellectual, or artistic talents will permit. In general, human beings have a need to marry and procreate, correlative with a duty to care for their children in love. Every person has a need to be free to some significant degree—as our sense of repugnance with respect to enslavement and oppression would indicate. And every human being has a need to find *and* to express meaning in life. Even the most cursory perusal of human history indicates that this pursuit of meaning usually involves a sense of harmony with the Creative Presence. With all of these needs come rights and duties. However varied the particular cultural manifestations of these rights and duties might be, all cultures attempt to organize themselves socially and institutionally in such a way as to meet these basic human needs, however imperfectly. Thus, the moral life unavoidably proceeds from essential needs to essential oughts.

The groundwork of natural law ethics is not to be found in the philosophical abstractions of the solitary mind. Natural law asks: What are the recognizable human goods that reasonably define basic well-being and flourishing? One way to answer this question is to make the most basic sorts of observations about the primary needs to which all well-ordered and thriving societies respond.

Every thriving society values the lives of its members and protects against the loss of life. This is why all societies invest in the training of competent physicians within some accepted system of medicine and value their efforts in saving life, caring for the infirm, and securing public health. Similarly, societies invest in fire departments, police forces, and defense. The high regard for those entrusted with health and safety is a manifestation of the first material content of natural law—that life itself is good and must be protected. While adverse human inclinations contrary to flourishing, such as wanton violence, can surface in any human society, they are proscribed rather than sanctioned.[4]

Every thriving society also values caring for and rearing children within the family context and with degrees of social support. *Abuse* and *neglect,* while admitting of some variation in definition across cultures, are universally terms of opprobrium. Every thriving society provides its young with educational opportunities required for vocational success within its resource range. It also provides sites for children to play and learn. No society that ignores the significance of the family as the central locus of child care and socialization, or that tolerates the neglect or abuse of children, can possibly thrive. Such societies exist, but they are not fully flourishing.

Every society fosters the expression of human creativity in the arts, cherishing works of great beauty in music, painting, sculpture, or writing. Such a society values educational institutions that allow people to learn about the world and contribute to it. A principle of natural law is that creative capacities must be encouraged and nurtured within a thriving society.

Similarly, every society includes religious symbols, rituals, and words to capture an essential and natural human propensity for a Creative Presence. These spiritual and religious opportunities need not be formally "established" or directly supported by the state, but the society must create the institutional settings that nurture this aspect of human nature. While there are some few who wish to utterly abolish any public mention or display of words or symbols that confirm in general terms the human inclination to live as "one nation under God," these efforts are akin to abolishing any public mention of the family, education, and health simply because some small minority objects to these values.

Few, if any, would seriously argue that *in thriving societies* respect for life and health, concern for the well-being of families and children, commitment to vocational training and education, cultivation of creativity, and respect for spiritual and religious expression are not centrally significant.

The ultimate question for natural law ethics and for any adequate ethics is this: What are the basic goods that contribute to human flourishing? While efforts to define these basic goods in a context of multicultural diversity sometimes seem futile, we must at least agree on some elements of a basic human good in order to have the minimal common vision necessary to sustain the political community. Of course, many societies over the course of history and in the present are regrettably unable to thrive, or are in decline from some earlier threshold of thriving, because one or more of these basic commensurable goods have been either ignored or undermined.

Among the Thomistic natural law theorists, the traditional understanding is that all the goods of human flourishing in this world are merely instrumental (i.e., having value only to the extent that they lead us to our transcendent ultimate end of friendship with the Supreme Being for eternity). Other Thomistic natural law theorists (Grisez, Boyle, and Finnis) believe these goods are ultimate ends in themselves.[5] My purpose is to explain how the eudaemonistic human propensity for worship of, and even love for, a Creative Presence figures into ethical theory and political philosophy, leading to a view of natural rights that includes, above all others, the right to freedom of spiritual-religious expression.

The Theory of Natural Law

To confirm the existence of a natural law morality, one has only to look at the basic goods in which societies invest and around which institutions are established and structured. Hospitals, schools, housing, playgrounds, museums and concert halls, and places for worship come immediately to mind. These basic goods are universal. To better explicate the theory of natural law, I turn here to some of its modern interpreters.

One of the modern defenders of natural law ethics is John Finnis of Oxford University. What does he believe are the universal features of human well-being? The first of seven basic human goods, "corresponding to the drive for self-preservation, is the value of life."[6] Finnis refers to medical schools, road safety laws, famine relief efforts, and the like as empirical evidence. The universal transmission of life through procreation and the rearing of children also establishes the human good of life itself. The second human good is knowledge, pursued not just instrumentally, but for its own sake.[7] While the noninstrumental pursuit of knowledge may reflect the ideals of an Oxford professor, knowledge for social and economic purposes is a universal human good. People need to take care of themselves and of others; to do so, they need some craft, trade, or other means of procuring necessities. A case can also be made for knowledge for its own sake, indicating the non-reducible feature of this human good. The third human good is play: "A certain sort of moralist analysing human goods may overlook this basic value, but an anthropologist will not fail to observe this large and irreducible element in human nature."[8] Is there a culture in which toys of some sort are unheard of, in which children play no games, in which some form of sport does not exist? A fourth human good is aesthetic experience. While many forms of play are occasions for aesthetic experience, Finnis argues that beauty is not an indispensable aspect of play; the experience of beauty need not involve one's own activity. The fifth basic human good is sociability and friendship. A sixth good is practical reasonableness, "the basic good of being able to bring one's own intelligence to bear effectively (in practical reasoning that issues in action) on the problems of choosing one's actions and lifestyle and shaping one's own character."[9] This good includes the good of freedom. The final good is religion:

> Misgivings may be aroused by the notion that one of the basic human values is the establishment and maintenance of proper relationships between oneself (and the orders one can create and maintain) and the divine. For there are, always, those who doubt or deny that the universal order-of-things has any origin beyond the "origins" known to the natural sciences.[10]

But Finnis argues persuasively that people do wish to bring their actions into harmony with "that transcendent other and its lasting order," even if they struggle in this effort and cannot ultimately achieve this harmony (as would be the case with Sartre).[11]

Finnis considers his list of the nonreducible basic human goods to be exhaustive, although other goods may combine elements of these seven:

Now besides life, knowledge, play, aesthetic experience, friendship, practical reasonableness, and religion, there are countless objectives and forms of good. But I suggest that these other objectives and forms of good will be found, on analysis, to be ways or combinations of ways of pursuing (not always sensibly) and realizing (not always successfully) one of the seven basic forms of good, or some combination of them.[12]

Further, the seven basic goods are all equally fundamental, although each person can reasonably determine to treat one good or several as of greater importance in his or her life. The ranking of goods is inevitably a subjective matter. While classic natural theory asks whether there is a hierarchy among the goods, I would contend that none of them can be set aside if full human flourishing is to be manifest.

The good of spirituality and religion is complex and can be discovered and pursued only if one is free from external constraint. The element of negative freedom is vitally important with regard to religion: a belief or act is free if the agent identifies with the elements from which it flows.[13] It is not inconsistent with this freedom to summarize the human goods as Finnis has done, creating an image that is so true to observed human experience that no reasonable person could contest it—even if at certain stages or times in life not everyone will deeply identify with all its elements. Natural law ethics is not draconian.

Finnis recognizes, as we all must, that human beings have all sorts of destructive inclinations that undermine human flourishing. The seven goods he has described are ones "that anyone intelligent would consider constitute human flourishing."[14] Moreover, Finnis concludes with a speculative argument that these forms of human flourishing reflect the wisdom of God, who is ultimately their creator. Human laws that violate these forms of flourishing are contrary to natural law and correlative natural rights. Human law should secure these goods, not impede them.

The critic might quibble with Finnis on the precise characterization of human goods. For example, would humor be worth mentioning as a subset of play? Should procreation be considered under its own category as a natural good, rather than being placed as a subset of the good of life? But few would fail to be refreshed by the recovery of the classical notion that ethics must be based on a consideration of the basic goods and needs of human nature. Anthony J. Lisska's analytic reconstruction of natural law ethics points out that twentieth-century moral philosophers have been caught up in hopeless abstractions because they forgot about the power and correctness of the rather basic observations of human flourishing. Lisska highlights the many logical errors of the philosophers' so-called "naturalistic fallacy"—that is, the assumption that began with Hume that one cannot derive "ought" from "is."[15] Even Hume, of course, derived his ethics from the human capacity to feel sympathy.

Hobbes and the contractarians had earlier developed an ethics of negative rules or philosophical "thou shalt nots," intended to ensure the human good of survival or what would correlate with the inclination to preserve life. Later, the utilitarians would base their ethical system on the good of happiness. However shallow these monistic notions of human good might be when compared with the rich plural view of human goods put forward by natural law theory, they are nevertheless "meta-ethically naturalistic." The alternative is a meta-ethical nonnaturalism summarized by G. E. Moore's statement that the good is an indefinable, simple, nonnatural property. Could anyone find this statement practically useful?

It is no surprise that Moore's abstraction led to the emotivist movement of A. J. Ayer and others, who claimed that all ethical statements are completely meaningless. This Anglo-American philosophical school dovetailed with the existentialism of Sartre, for whom there were no essential human goods and, therefore, no ethics other than what the individual invents for the moment. In the context of a potent denunciation of much of modern moral philosophy, Alasdair MacIntyre states that we must ask these sorts of questions again: "What is the *telos* of human beings? What is right action directed toward the *telos?* What are the virtues which issue in right action?"[16] MacIntyre asks philosophers to turn their attention in a grounded way to the universal goods associated with well-ordered and flourishing lives. Strauss wrote that human excellence flows from living according to nature, inclusive of all the constructive human capacities and tendencies. For example, "Man is by nature a social being. He is so constituted that he cannot live, or live well, except by living with others."[17] Natural law, argues Strauss, is a kind of full flowering that requires the free pursuit of excellence, not the proverbial hedonic naturalism.

As one walks down Woodstock Road in Oxford, one sees a playground, St. Anthony's College, the Radcliff Infirmary, a beautiful church, and a restaurant where friends gather. What thriving city does not invest in competent physicians or nurses, agriculture, and housing? What thriving city does not invest in schools, museums, libraries, concert halls, and theaters? Here is the good of intellectual and artistic creativity and aesthetic experience. What thriving city does not invest in families, children, and industry? Here is the good of the young and of future generations. What thriving city does not make room for synagogues, churches, or other places of worship and allude to spiritual and religious inclination as important? Despite the confusion of some ethicists, the investment in the essential human goods continues.

The notion of religion as a basic human good might be questioned on some superficial level in the heavily intellectual milieu of Oxford, where fair numbers of churches have been transformed into restaurants or institutes. Yet people in this city of critical thinkers are still seeking meaning and wanting to find order and orientation in the world. They still want to have faith in the future of the universe, and they still, for the most part, seriously debate and often accept the notion of a presence in the universe that is greater than our own. The search for ultimate reality and Creative Presence does not die, although it transposes into different forms as external institutions wax and wane.

A regrettable feature of the Western Enlightenment was that it replaced natural law, replete with its Aristotelian and Thomistic attentiveness to objective and essential human goods, with a "state of nature" that was supposedly in existence prior to the state of society; the Enlightenment supported only a very limited concept of natural rights as a result. The classical ethics of natural law, however, began with a full accounting of the essential nature of the human—including the mind of God that lay mysteriously behind this nature. In contrast, Hobbes's state of nature was merely a state of selfishness and chaos that was repressed by the absolute law of the sovereign Leviathan. In Hobbes's revision, as Heinrich Rommen states, "The older idea of natural law as an ethical system with material contents loses all its function; namely, to serve as a moral basis for positive law."[18] In the theories of Hobbes and Locke, *nature* refers not to essential human nature but to a fictitious epoch in history. René Descartes could describe essential human nature only as *res cogitans,* a being that thinks. Human reason becomes the sovereign architect of the moral for Kant, in contrast to the natural law tradition in which practical reason desciphers embodied human nature in the *ordo rerum* (order of things). Kant's disembodied and denatured reason renders the objective order of nature and of human nature superfluous. His reason gives no attention to essential goods and needs, except insofar as rationality itself is the essential capacity. As Rommen sums up the problem, "The objective basis of natural law, the *ordo rerum* and the eternal law, has vanished. What was termed natural law is a series of conclusions drawn from the categorical imperative and from regulative ideas of practical reason, not from the objective and constitutive *ordo rerum.*"[19] God, human nature, and ethics are severed, except perhaps in the most tangential ways.[20].

Responses to the standard critique of natural law ethics are mixed. One example of such a critique is Reinhold Niebuhr's: "Undue confidence in human reason, as the seat and source of natural law, makes this very concept of law into a vehicle of human sin. It gives the peculiar conditions and unique circumstances in which reason operates in a particular historical moment, the sanctity of universality."[21] Niebuhr adds that the "pretensions of the age" and "contingent factors" are made into "fixed socio-ethical principles."[22] Such criticisms are valuable, since there is a powerful tendency to absolutize the values of one's own culture and time, even to the point of associating them with the timeless features of one's religious tradition. This leads to the perennial problem of the religion of culture—the use of religion to sanctify all the moral and social errors of one's culture in order to avoid serious self-critical reflection. Niebuhr mentions the absolutizing of patriarchy as an example of oppression writ sacred in natural law. Such suspicions must be valued. As Niebuhr warns, "the premature fixation of certain historical standards in regard to the family will inevitably tend to reinforce male arrogance and to retard justified efforts on the part of the female to achieve such freedom."[23]

Niebuhr's line of argument is rather consistent with deconstructionism, which sees in any cultural images of essential human flourishing the abuse of power in the forms of patriarchy, discrimination, and oppression. Such critiques must be taken with seriousness and the imposition of such images avoided by ensuring pluralism under constitutional rights. Deconstructionism goes too far, however, when it claims that any description of the human good is to be utterly avoided as an affront to negative freedom. I agree with Foucault that images of the human good can be used in politically oppressive ways, but I do not think that this is inevitable. Deconstructionism is a necessary corrective voice that forces anyone espousing normative ethics of natural law to protect freedoms, emancipation, and liberations.[24] Ultimately, however, deconstructionism errs when it implies that nothing can be agreed upon with regard to basic well-being.

Criticism of natural law goes too far when it diminishes all confidence in reasonable observations about human flourishing. We can still speak of essential human goods that fulfill, rather than harm, self and society. The alternative is sheer moral relativism.[25] Even Niebuhr observes that there are still "certain permanent norms, such as monogamy," which are consistent with "the cumulative experience of the race."[26] Practically speaking, one approach to avoiding the absolutizing of the relative is to engage in community dialogues around notions of human flourishing. There will be a general agreement on such goods as decent food, safety, health care, family, education, peace, and freedom of spiritual or religious expression. The psychologist Abraham Maslow set out the basic outlines of a theory of basic human needs with their correlative goods in his famous hierarchy of bodily, intellectual, emotional, social, and religious needs.

In a world of dramatic pluralism and diversity, any claims about essential human goods require a foundation in empirical data. Thus, in the preceding chapter, I presented various studies on the benefits of religion in the context of serious illness. Natural law theorists must provide evidence for their claims about general human flourishing; unlike most other ethical theories, the goods of natural law can be empirically assessed and verified, for the facts of flourishing are not separated from values.

For example, natural law theorists have classically made claims about marriage and procreation. But the theorists rarely take advantage of empirical findings, and they leave themselves open to the sort of radical deconstructionist assault which states that there are absolutely no essential human goods. These claims about the general good of marriage and of the presence of both parents in child rearing are much questioned today, just as the notion of *Homo religiosus* might be. Thus it is important to invoke social scientific data.

For example, a great deal of demographic evidence indicates that marital disruption contributes to mortality rates, but this is not our epidemiological focus.[27] Beginning in the early 1970s, Judith S. Wallerstein's longitudinal studies of families undergoing divorce found that the adverse psychological consequences of marital breakup were considerable for both adults and children.[28] In particular, Wallerstein's studies challenged the then current assumption that exposure to degrees of low-level conflict and disharmony in parental relationships is worse for children than the experience of family breakup through divorce. Her work is now widely regarded as scientifically valid. At the time of publication, however, she was ridiculed mercilessly by critics who did not wish to admit the adverse consequences of the rising divorce curve. In their fifteen-year study of divorce, Wallerstein and Sandra Blakeslee found that only 10 percent of children felt better about their lives after parental divorce.[29] After five years, more than a third of these children were suffering from clinical depression; after ten years, unusually high numbers were underachievers; after fifteen years, disproportionate numbers were insecure and struggling to establish stable relationships themselves. By the mid-1980s, researchers across the United States were backing away from two decades of optimism regarding the effects of divorce on children.

The harm is not limited to children. Divorced or separated persons, especially men, are disproportionately represented among psychiatric patients.[30] The medical literature abounds with studies indicating that divorce is generally a stressful event that is associated with physical and psychological adverse consequences.[31] While remarriages are common, they are complex and difficult for children, who often find them to be no substitute for the original family.[32] Researchers are now pointing out that stepfamilies present their own set of unique difficulties for children.[33] After reviewing extensive data, Martin Daly and Margo Wilson report that stepparents generally care "less profoundly for children than natural parents."[34] These are, of course, general data and should not be used as criteria for individual cases. The authors found that fatal child abuse was 100 times more likely in stepfamilies. In their monumental study of current data, Sara McLanahan and Gary Sandefur conclude that children in stepfamilies benefit from family incomes that are equivalent to those of the formerly intact families. Nonetheless, they are also two to three times more likely to have behavioral and emotional problems than children in still-intact families, twice as likely to have developmental or learning problems, more likely to drop out of high school, more likely to become single teenage mothers, and less able to hold steady jobs as young adults.[35] These authors find that children may be better off with divorce in cases of high-level persistent conflict between parents; in cases of low-level conflict, emotional distancing, boredom, or a change in one spouse's priorities, however, children would be better off if parents resolved their difficulties and stayed together.[36]

It appears that the optimum good of children requires a two-parent situation; if this is unavailable, alternative supportive networks are important for filling the gaps. The above discussion of the human good of marriage in relation to procreation contained no abstract statements. The question is whether the facts support the claim of a moral good. Similarly, in the area of religious propensity, the preceding chapter included evidence of firm measurable benefits to spirituality and religion in the context of health care and psychological well-being. Any theory of natural law is, of course, subject to revision should new facts be discovered or old assumptions falsified.

Classically, the ethics of natural law was thought to reflect the creative ordering and purposes of the Creative Presence. God, human nature, and ethics were all points on the same triangle. John Courtney Murray defines natural law with respect to four principles that are worth quoting in full:

> The whole metaphysic involved in the idea of natural law may seem alarmingly complicated; in a sense it is. Natural law presupposes a realist epistemology, that asserts the real to be the measure of knowledge, and also asserts the possibility of intelligence reaching the real, i.e., the nature of things — in this case, the nature of man as a unitary and constant concept beneath all individual differences. Secondly, it supposes a metaphysic of nature, especially the idea that nature is a teleological concept, the "form" of a thing is its "final cause," the goal of its becoming; in this case, that there is a natural inclination in man to become what in nature and destination he is — to achieve the fullness of his own being. Thirdly, it supposes a natural theology, asserting that there is a God, Who is eternal Reason, *Nous,* at the summit of the order of being, Who is the author of all nature, and Who wills that the order of nature be fulfilled in all its purposes, as these are inherent in the natures found in the order. Finally, it supposes a morality, especially the principle that for man, a rational being, the order of nature is not an order of necessity, to be fulfilled blindly, but an order of reason and therefore of freedom. The order

of being that confronts his intelligence is an order of "oughtness" for his will; the moral order is a prolongation of the metaphysical order into the dimension of human freedom.[37]

The first principle is that, after sustained reflection on the dynamics of human action, we can actually know what the various human goods are. Second, on some level, the human self wants to realize the fullness of its being and generally strives to do so if given the chance. Third, that fullness of being somehow reflects the Author of being. Fourth, the human person participates in the natural law by free will, not by force or any form of coercion. The person is perfectly free *not* to pursue all the goods of natural law. Any individual human being may have various emotional and physical particularities that require a focus on some set of goods rather than others. Or an individual may wish to defy the natural law, although ultimately this will not lead to full flourishing, even if the life lived is to relative degrees satisfactory.

Naturally Inclined Toward a Creative Presence?
The Secular Existentialist Alternative

The discussion of *Homo religiosus* is important because, as philosopher Leslie Stevenson argues, "different views about human nature lead naturally to different conclusions about what we ought to do and how we can do it. If God made us, then it is His purpose that defines what we ought to be, and we must look to Him for help."[38] Stevenson emphasizes that views of human nature are invariably informed by some prior view of the nature of the universe. Whether religious, Marxist, behaviorist, or sociobiological, all the theories of human nature have in common four elements: "(1) a background theory of the nature of the universe; (2) a basic theory of the nature of man;

(3) a diagnosis of what is wrong with man; and (4) a prescription for putting it right."[39]

One portrait of human nature, secular existentialism, that appeals to relatively few over the long course of life's journey makes no reference to a Creative Presence. Often its proponents are not deeply informed Sartreans—they are the sort of "easy existentialists" who want Sartre's results but lack Sartre's dismay at a world without God or religion. Some observers define western Europe as a post-Christian culture, but few define it as a postspiritual culture because belief in God is anything but dead. Only an estimated 10 percent of the English attend church regularly, which may be due to the adverse effects of established national religion. In a downward trajectory from 1991, regular church attendance is at 7 percent for West Germans, 4.1 percent for Norwegians, 29.4 percent for Italians, and 63.2 percent for Irish.[40] George Carey, the archbishop of Canterbury, warned that the Church of England is "one generation away from extinction." Many Europeans, especially after a series of events in Ireland, see the church as a shelter for sexual hypocrisy. A certain extrinsic religiosity continues to serve social expectations, as in baptism, marriage, and funerals. *Yet despite a strong anticlericalism among the middle-aged and a flat indifference in the young, 90 percent of Europeans believe in God and religious books become best-sellers.*[41] So this is a time of perceiving a Creative Presence, but not one of belonging to organized religions. Thus the human inclination toward this Presence outlasts the collapse of institutional religion in western Europe, where, in contrast to many other parts of the world, organized religion has declined rather considerably.[42]

In comparison to the now defunct Marxism, Stevenson writes that an "existentialist" philosophy like Sartre's may at first seem less likely to guide social practice. In fact, he argues, this is not true.[43] Secular existentialism justifies the view that religious persons should express themselves in private but never in public and that the only permissible language of public debate must be secular. Sartre was, of course, not asserting that human nature has no religious impulse; like Nietzsche, he was first asserting God's nonexistence and a consequent sense of life in the barren universe as "absurd" and "forlorn." From this perspective on the nature of the universe, Sartre's view of human nature is not that it is devoid of religious impulses. Rather, he believes that these impulses should not be taken as veridical when we know that they are not so (though natural, religious impulses lead to "bad faith" or inauthenticity). Freud too was impressed by the pervasiveness and power of the natural religious impulse even as he wished to see this impulse inhibited by reason.

Secular existentialism may offer a new degree of human freedom from all objective norms, but is not a worldview that gives much meaning to our lives. For both Nietzsche and Sartre, the denial of a Creative Presence is the most important metaphysical assertion. They come to atheism by affirming human freedom as absolute. (For Sartre, freedom is not an idea to be achieved but a fact to be acknowledged; there is no universe but only being-in-itself, which is differentiated only by the negating activity of consciousness in being-for-itself.) Their assertion of God's nonexistence was simply a prelude to the main question of what such a denial meant for human nature and human existence. For Sartre, the only basis for moral values is human freedom to create *ex nihilo* whatever values it happens to think, in the throes of malaise and whim, are worth asserting for the moment. There is no rational sense of wonder over the gift of life in a mysteriously generative universe and an improbably pregnant earth. Because there is no sense of the divine gift of life, there is finally no affirmation of spiritual and moral stewardship over that life. The notion that every human is worthy of our celebration and care evaporates. We are only "condemned to be free," with no way of life to be recommended and no respite from hopeless malaise. I recall vividly attending a performance of *Waiting for Godot* as a high school boy and leaving with much dampened enthusiasm for life.

Not incidentally, there is a rather unclear and acrimonious debate about whether Sartre was more open to theism in his last years. In 1980, with Sartre blind, near death, but still very lucid, the French journal *Nouvel Observateur* published a dialogue between Sartre and the ex-Maoist Pierre Victor. At least for a fleeting moment, Sartre *may* have come close to a theistic position with these words: "I do not feel that I am the product of chance, a speck of dust in the universe, but someone who was expected, prepared, prefigured. In short, a being whom only a Creator could put here; and the idea of a creating hand refers to God."[44] Various militant atheists, including Simone de Beauvoir, claimed that somehow Victor had seduced Sartre into this statement. But it seems at least as likely that a blind old man came to see. We will never know for sure if he was ever truly free from what he had earlier described as "nausea," the sense of disgust over one's own very existence that follows from meaninglessness and that even his later neo-Marxism could not fend off.[45] Yet his transition suggests that human beings may not have evolved in Bertrand Russell's uncaring objective universe, where we are, objectively speaking, insignificant.

It is, I believe, not sufficiently well appreciated that great secularist philosophers such as Sartre and Russell did themselves struggle with the religious impulse. The early Russell, for instance, insisted on a religion consistent with science; like Plato, he took seriously the idea that mathematics disclosed a stable universal order and ordering being. It is true that the later Russell set aside the religion of reason and came to be extremely critical of the role of religion in civilization. Yet he still wrote of a sense of cosmic piety against a technological imperative, and he shaped his affective being on the basis of a powerful conversion moment of "self-enlargement" through compassion.[46] His profound thoughts on an affect of other-regarding love and compassion consistent with the grain of the cosmos would today fall loosely into the rather amorphous category of spirituality.

Even as they asserted an agnostic or atheistic worldview, great minds such as Sartre or Russell had to nevertheless seriously grapple with the human religious impulse. The power of the human sense of a Creative Presence could not be denied, no matter how it might be analyzed, dismissed, and inhibited. Such admittedly great minds must be contrasted with the "easy" secularists of today who unthinkingly assert the unreality of that Being. As the twenty-first century begins, the religious impulse, strong as it is, has hardly been dampened. So perhaps there really is something to the idea of an essential human impulse, essential because it evolved in response to the objective presence of that Creative Presence. This statement raises certain questions of a scientific sort.

Secular existentialism is strongly reinforced by scientific interpretations of reality that assert the meaninglessness of religious views of the cosmos, nature, and human nature. While European churches are being converted into restaurants and art galleries, Karen Armstrong notes that people in Europe are nevertheless again keenly interested in religious questions. She believes that Christianity will have to change in many ways to speak to these questions. Armstrong makes this telling comment about western European youth raised in a context of scientific positivism:

> In the premodern world, it was generally understood that while reason was indispensable for mathematics, science or politics, it could not, by itself, give human beings access to the divine. But the extraordinary success of scientific

rationalism in the modern world has made reason the only path to truth. We assume that God is an objective fact, like the atom, whose existence can be proved empirically. When we find the demonstration unconvincing, we lose faith. Our neglect of the aesthetic of prayer, liturgy and mythology has indeed "killed" our sense of the divine.[47]

Actually, the importance of rational demonstration for the retrieval of theism is anything but purely modern. The Greek philosophers, especially Aristotle, thought that reason gives us access to the divine (of course, with no notion of creation, we do not get a god to be worshiped but only one to be contemplated).[48] Armstrong's suggestion that the rapprochement between science and religion has potential as a path to truth points to a renewed sense that religion is, for many of us, including myself, highly rational.

Is there an essential inclination toward a Creative Presence that, if fulfilled, enhances human life? Can this be demonstrated empirically? One goal of the earlier discussion of health and illness was to begin to demonstrate the role of scientific studies in this area. Over the last decade, a remarkable empirical literature has emerged indicating that in the circumstances of coping with a serious illness, it is part of human nature to look toward a Creative Presence. The evidence is both grounded in an experiential epistemology and carefully analyzed according to the best social scientific and epidemiological methods. For most people, a sense of cosmic purpose is *essential* for personal meaning—and it is a *serious* matter to lose the sense that the universe has a purpose. Human beings seem to have evolved a capacity to sense a Creative Presence that they perceive is a way out of despair and meaninglessness. Such a capacity should be respected under the rubric of natural rights.

From Natural Law to Natural Rights

Any natural rights are isomorphic with essential human goods (and therefore needs) as defined by a reasonable view of human flourishing. There are rights to be left free of interference ("negative rights") and rights to those resources that are conducive to flourishing ("positive rights"). In the latter category, we may speak of rights to at least a decent minimum of nutrition, health care, housing, and education. Although religious freedom of expression is typically thought of as a negative right, I view it as both a negative and a positive right. On the negative side, there is a right to be left alone to pursue religious truth as one sees that truth, to speak publicly as one wishes, and to act accordingly within the limits of law; on the positive side, government and law must set conditions that allow for the free expression of religion, rather than conditions that inhibit it.

The correlation between essential human goods and rights is important. If we deny that X is a human good, it need not be taken seriously as either a negative or a positive right. People cannot justly claim rights to those things that are not required for human flourishing. For example, if education is dismissed as being inessential to flourishing, we have no need for or right to public schools. But we do think that there is a positive right to education, even at higher levels—although this entails access to the state university and not to Harvard. We think that there is a positive right to reasonable health care—hence, the National Health Service in Great Britain or the health care safety net in the United States. We ought to take rights to food and housing much more seriously. The moral, political, and economic challenge of positive rights is that they create a correlative obligation on the part of others (society) to accommodate them.

Negative rights center on matters of privacy and conscience. If we do not see privacy and confidentiality as essential, we have

George Orwell's *1984,* in which Big Brother peers all-knowingly into every detail of every life. Such a society is aptly described as dystopian. If we do not see religion as essential to human flourishing, we can easily dismiss it. If religion is deemed non-essential, no special rights attach to it. Such ideas may, in some social contexts, have consequences. Marx believed that religion, merely the subjective "opiate of the people," is inessential and ultimately will die out because social justice and equality will be achieved in the "people's paradise." Thus, in the former USSR, there was no freedom of religious belief, practice, or public speech. The positivist Freudian assumption that religion is purely "illusion" meant that it had no future; therefore, Freudian psychiatrists allowed no religious ideation on the part of patients in the clinical environment.

Natural law and natural rights do not arise abstractly from reason alone; they result from reflections on the intelligible goods and necessities that correspond to the essential human constitution. Cultures may meet these basic needs in many ways, and some cultures may fail to meet some of them entirely. While scientific knowledge has the potential to better clarify some of these basic needs and rights, most are already obvious. For example, an obvious good of human nature is the preservation of being. Because human beings have a right to live, our collective repugnance toward the various genocides and other hate crimes is pronounced.

In the words of Maritain,

> The same natural law which lays down our most fundamental duties, and by virtue of which every law is binding, is the very law which assigns us our fundamental rights. It is because we are enmeshed in the universal order, in the laws and regulations of the cosmos and of the immense family of created natures (and finally in the order of creative wisdom), and it is because we have at the same time the privilege of

sharing in spiritual nature, that we possess rights vis-a-vis other men and all the assemblage of creatures.[49]

Ultimately, we possess rights because the emergence of our natures reflects the cosmic work of a Creative Presence. The human person in his or her relation to a Creative Presence transcends the body politic; therefore, no society can rightfully subordinate these relational interests. Maritain speaks of "the primacy of the spiritual."[50] Contrary to the secular philosophers, most people believe that moral values spring from spiritual values. Religion should have no domination over the body politic, but it should be allowed full freedom within the body politic. There should be no establishment of a religion or of religions, but the free exercise of religions should be an established and celebrated fact.

CHAPTER FOUR

Religious Inclinations
in the Public Square

As noted earlier, the capacity for spirituality and religion is somewhat like the capacity for language, which seems to "come naturally" in the sense that human beings everywhere have it and rely on it, even though the specific symbol system may vary and cultural learning is often involved. This capacity is selectively adaptive for a species aware of its frailty and for which a relationship with a Creative Presence seems to bring more lasting security and peace. To forbid a person from publicly expressing spiritual and religious values, from which his or her moral and political values are emergent, is not unlike forbidding the exercise of a person's capacity for speech. Such silencing is a grave imposition. The harms of forced religious silence are self-evident, including the experiences of invalidation and disempowerment. Even indifference to the religious voice is a form of disdain. Yet some very prominent and influential political philosophers appear to advocate such silencing, either fully or for the most part. It is necessary to introduce their ideas and critique them, as well as to point out that the perspective they espouse is entirely resonant with the endeavor to censor the religious perspective from the schools. I then turn more broadly to the immense historic value of particularistic religious expression in public debate and to its potential contribution to civility in public discourse, underscoring that contrary to the prejudices of those who would exclude, this voice is in general publicly beneficial and creatively idealistic.

Political Philosophers of Exclusion

The philosopher Richard Rorty contends that religious expression should be entirely privatized and excluded from all political and public discourse. Religion should be a purely internal affair, no more relevant to public discourse than one's culinary tastes. When religious voices are allowed to speak, the result is only a harsh discordant mixture of chaotic sounds that mean nothing. He therefore recommends a common secular language.[1] Rorty, ironically the grandson of the Social Gospel theologian Walter Rauschenbusch, has written an essay entitled "Religion as Conversation-Stopper," in which he describes "secularization of public life as the Enlightenment's central achievement."[2] He describes himself as "puzzled and amazed" by critics of the privatization of religion.[3] Indeed, Rorty goes so far as to proclaim for himself a mission of "making it seem bad taste to bring religion into discussions of public policy."[4] In attacking the arguments of Stephen L. Carter, Rorty writes, "Carter's inference from privatization to trivialization is invalid unless supplemented by the premise that the nonpolitical is always trivial. But this premise seems false."[5]

Rorty's harsh privatization, however, cannot be separated from trivialization quite so easily, as this chapter will show. In a widely cited line, Rorty lays out his simplistic view of the religious voice: "The main reason religion needs to be privatized is that, in political discussion with those outside the relevant religious community, it is a conversation-stopper."[6] Some religious voices *are* conversation stoppers, no doubt. But so are many secular voices. Moreover, a great many religious voices are respectful, diplomatic, and contributory to deeper levels of discourse on public issues. They are as much, or more, conversation starters than conversation stoppers. Yet Rorty will not acknowledge anything other than his negative "stopper" metaphor. A political leftist, Rorty must be aware that often the most liberal and socialistic voices in American reform have been religious.

Rorty does state that religious premises will certainly influence the statements of citizens, but this influence must be entirely beneath the surface of democratically suitable political discussion. Pity the students in his classes at the University of Virginia should they conclude that the available suitable discourse cannot capture their positions. Rorty's democracy therefore is not consistent with pluralistic liberal democracy—it is a democracy in which ideally only people who speak more or less exactly like him should utter a word. This, of course, is no democracy at all.

While Rorty is especially aggressive in his position, he is representative of a larger set of political philosophers who would follow his inclination toward censorship. Bruce Ackerman, to mention another example from the ranks of elite political philosophy, explicitly states that all decision making in a liberal democracy should be entirely "rational," a requirement that rules out the religious voice.[7] Like Rorty, he also stereotypes religious individuals as being psychologically incapable of democratic discourse and compromise, as though the same could not be said for persons with strong secular moral convictions, such as the representatives of labor unions, the National Organization for Women, or homosexual rights groups such as Act-Up.

A somewhat less strident secularism is expressed by John Rawls, who contends that statements not articulable within the confines of "public reason" should not enter into public debates. Any particularistic moral convictions drawn from faith and ethnic traditions should be censored. They can be articulated only through translation, when possible, into properly public reasons. In essence, religious moral views must be robustly privatized. For Rawls, it is as if diversity, both cultural and religious and linguistic, need not be taken very seriously. Consensus, or at least the mirage of consensus, must be achieved without real dialogue and real conversation between those true to their own values and language. Illusory consensus takes the place of democracy's time-honored tradition of *Realpolitik* negotiation between those whose views really do differ. Rawls has, however, moved toward a very circumscribed acceptance of religious language in the public square and is thus not as constricting as is Rorty. Rawls is worth quoting at some length:

> The Fact of Public Reason: This is the fact that citizens in a pluralist liberal democratic society realize that they cannot reach agreement, or even approach mutual understanding, on the basis of their irreconcilable comprehensive doctrines. Thus, when citizens are discussing fundamental political questions, they appeal not to those doctrines, but to a reasonable family of political conceptions of right and justice, and so to the idea of the politically reasonable addressed to citizens as citizens. This does not mean that doctrines of faith or nonreligious (secular) doctrines cannot be introduced into political discussion, but rather that citizens introducing them should also provide sufficient grounds in public reason for the political policies that religious or nonreligious doctrines support.[8]

It is, of course, a burden for religious voices to translate themselves into the secular principles and language of public reason. Moreover, just because such translation may not in each instance be possible should not imply that the religious voice is

inessential to the well-being of the republic. Indeed, it is sometimes just precisely when the religious voice is asserted despite
the limits of the current secular discourse that positive social
change can occur—for example, in the antislavery movement
or civil rights protests. Of course antislavery eventually came to
be defended on the grounds of rational principle and public
reason, but its origins lie firmly with antebellum Protestant
abolitionists. I will acknowledge that when the secular language
of the Republic does allow for translation to occur from religious first principles, there may sometimes be a strategic value
in appealing to such language along with the particularistic
features of the religious framework of relevance. Nevertheless,
Rawls does impose a wall of silence on the prophetic religious
voice, however qualified.

Rawls tries to be more respectful of religion than Rorty, but
his success is not overwhelming. He comments that religion
should not be trivialized by overexpression for political ends:
"Political liberalism does not dismiss spiritual questions as un-
important, but to the contrary, because of their importance, it
leaves them for each citizen to decide for himself or herself.
This is not to say that religion is somehow 'privatized'; instead,
it is not 'politicized' (that is, perverted and diminished for ideological ends)."[9] I would prefer to him to make the slightly different point that religion will always have its ethical and political implications, which citizens are free to voice, but should
they appeal to religious perspective too often they run the risk
of trivializing their perspective through overuse and firm comment on issues about which their traditions are unclear or
divided to begin with. It surely is a pity when those represent-
ing any religious tradition feel that they must direct the resources of that tradition to each issue of the day, even when the
tradition itself is neither much concerned with the issue or particularly vivid about it. But this is not what Rawls is saying. His

point seems to be that the religious voice in the political arena somehow diminishes the purity of religiosity. This point is baseless, for there is nothing impure about speaking out.

In the final analysis, Rawls still fails to see that the religious voice, usually an ethnoreligious voice, can and should be heard in public debate over the good of the commonweal. It is not clear that he has moved away from the biases of his earlier writing.[10] In his lengthy introduction to *Political Liberalism* (1993), in which religion is considered in depth, Rawls does not show any disrespect for religious or other voluntary associations. However, he works with an image of "mortal combat," like that between Catholics and Protestants in the religious wars of the Reformation period.[11] With this backdrop of a distant history of violence between "salvationist, creedal, and expansionist religions," Rawls prescribes as a solution the common rational language of justice that is essentially his life's philosophical work.[12] He asks: "How is it possible for those affirming a religious doctrine that is based on religious authority, for example, the Church or the Bible, also to hold a reasonable political conception that supports a just democratic regime?"[13]

Michael Walzer would never ask such a Rawlsian question because he understands the creative place of tension between the one and the many—or, in other words, between "thin" publicly accessible language and ethnoreligious particularity, in the public square. Walzer offers a useful perspective on the tension in a remarkable "thick" and "thin" discourse.[14] The language of the "thin" is also the language of the one, the narrow band of consensus that moves across cultures to form a universal-of-a-sort. The allowable appeals are to social scientific data and to general principles (such as nonmaleficence, autonomy, and justice) outside any historical or culturally specific context. Rorty and Rawls abide by the laws of thinness that either entirely or in large part eliminate ethnoreligious "thick" language.[15] Walzer sees very limited value in this thin endeavor, for too much thickness and reality are lost in the process; ultimately, thinness both demeans the religious voice and is unsatisfying to all but its devisers. *Most significantly, the image of thin moral consensus within a universalist language game largely misrepresents the very process by which consensus is achieved, for moral consensus does not precede dialogue. Rather, it is the result of real dialogue between real people with all their ethnoreligious thickness.* This is not to say that thin moral consensus cannot be had on certain matters such as the prohibitions of rape and murder, but even these emerge from innumerable particular traditions and are found to be held more or less in common. In other words, the thin consensus is inductive after the method, for example, of a focus group of particular individuals who, from their various ethnoreligious frameworks, discover that they do after all arrive at similar conclusions.

Walzer does an effective job of describing the *real* nature of political discourse in a liberal democracy:

> The order of the self is better imagined as a thickly populated circle, with me in the center surrounded by my self-critics who stand at different temporal and spatial removes (but don't necessarily stand still). Insofar as I am receptive to criticism, ready for (a little) castigation, I try to draw some of the critics closer, so that I am more immediately aware of their criticism. . . . My inner world is full of givens, too, culturally bestowed or socially imposed—I maneuver among them insofar as their plurality allows for the maneuvering. . . . This at least is the thick view of the self.[16]

There is here no dominance of a single voice, not even a secular voice, but a participation in full by all. Walzer envisions a thick and respectful discourse that builds on thick particularism rather than silences it.

The question arises: While certain secular philosophers wish to invalidate the religious and ethnic voice in the public square, are they not merely speaking to one another in a fairly esoteric circle divorced from the thick realities of democratic life? Have they not forgotten the epistemology of what anthropologist Clifford Geertz refers to as "local knowledge," or the reality that people's understanding of events is intractably grounded in the intimacies of their local world?[17] No matter how academically influential Rorty and Rawls are, they may be so far removed from the real world of political discourse in America, which is historically deeply religious, as to be more or less irrelevant. Rorty and Rawls seem singularly uninterested in the voices of those as politically significant as Lincoln or Rev. Martin Luther King, Jr. In this sense, their philosophical construction of political liberalism is disconnected from the realities of American democratic history and experience. One must, then, honestly ask if responding to these philosophers has anything other than merely academic value. Probably not.

But how do the vast majority of citizens who cherish religious beliefs simply take them off as one would discard dirty clothes before a purifying shower? Certainly Rorty and, to a large extent, Rawls seem to think that religious reasons are disposable items. A believer who is working to participate meaningfully and creatively within the public policy context, abiding by the rules of civility, pluralism, and respect, will be offended, and rightly so. It is worth noting that for all that light of the Enlightenment, its Kantian notion of "perpetual peace" was based on the exclusion of religious identity. Thus, the Enlightenment always had, as Roy Porter writes, a "dark side"—namely, it was the fruit of an elitist mentality that held "the masses in contempt," especially with regard to any religious expression.[18]

This assertion that only secular monism—the view that only arguments completely free of religious principles or appeals— can contribute to debates over the common good reveals an absolutist overtone. Daniel O. Conkle, for example, describes a "secular fundamentalism" that "depends on faith, that shields itself from incompatible truth claims, and that effectively isolates itself as a separate system of thought."[19] He identifies this with Rawls, in whose system appeal to "reason" as he defines it assumes the role of sacred scripture, as if images of "the reasonable" in his own system were not deeply colored by historical particularities. Rawls, in his willingness to deny others the moral language of their choice, is remarkably intolerant despite his claim that tolerance and pluralism are key goals of political liberalism. Conkle rightly points out the informed and rational aspects of most religious discourse of significance on social issues. In the final analysis, if fundamentalism is defined as the denial of epistemic diversity, then Rawls, Rorty, and Ackerman qualify. As Michael J. Perry writes, "Undeniably, some religious believers are unable to gain much if any critical distance on their fundamental religious beliefs. As so much in the twentieth century attests, however, one need not be a religious believer to adhere to one's fundamental beliefs with closed-minded or even fanatical tenacity."[20] Perry finds no reason to believe that religious contributions to public debate are nondeliberative or irrational:

> Because of the religious illiteracy—and, alas, even prejudice—rampant among many nonreligious intellectuals, we probably need reminding that, at its best, religious discourse in public culture is not less dialogic—not less open-minded, not less deliberative—than is, at its best, secular discourse in public culture. (Nor, at its worst, is religious discourse more monologic—more closed-minded and dogmatic—than is, at its worst, secular discourse.)[21]

I am in full agreement with Perry when he argues that "we should simply welcome the presentation of religiously based moral arguments in *all* areas of our public culture, *including* public debate specifically about contested political choices. Indeed, we should not merely welcome but *encourage* the presentation of such arguments in public political debate[22]—so that we can test them there." I would also agree with Perry that religious voices usually *should* attempt to appeal to reason, as well as exercise some degree of self-restraint, but that *contrary* to Rawls, this cannot be made a requirement of participation in public debate—for such a requirement is a form of censorship that undermines the very dialogic nature of open democratic discourse.

Thinkers such as Rorty and Rawls write for a future that will never happen, for the core component of a liberal society is that no particular voice should be publicly privileged. Theorists of secularization may have posited a future in which the role of religious expression would decrease in the public square. The distorted image of political liberalism that these philosophers put forward provides a certain abstract philosophical support for a future that they seem to advocate. But empirically, secularization is nothing but a myth—perhaps the greatest myth of the last century. In fact, religious expression remains vivid, emboldened, and present in increasing diversity. In this fact is testimony to the reality of *Homo religiosus*. I find much to agree with in Richard John Neuhaus's statement that "in a democracy that is free and robust, an opinion is no more disqualified for being 'religious' than for being atheistic, or psychoanalytic, or Marxist, or just plain dumb."[23] There really is no constitutional or legal issue, argues Neuhaus, because "religion in public is but the public opinion of those citizens who are religious."[24]

The Implications of Secular Monism in the Schools: Why Vouchers?

The assumption that secular monism must reign in meaningful public discourse is erroneous not only in the public square but also in the public schools. Indeed, the mistaken insistence on secular monism in the schools contributes to the diminished vitality of political discourse. If people are to speak well and respectfully from the perspective of their faith traditions, thereby keeping their sacred values intact, they need to be taught to do so through educational opportunities designed to enhance real tolerance and respect—not the false tolerance and respect that comes with silencing the religious voice. But if the public schools—an ideal site for respectful dialogue between people of different traditions—refuse to allow students of faith to fully participate in discussion through bringing their deepest commitments to the table, then this education cannot occur. The result may be that when such students participate in civic discourse as adults, they have not yet fully learned how to conduct themselves, nor how to respect the views of faith traditions other than their own.

In the public schools, but also in our public and private colleges and universities, the message is that religion must be privatized, that it can have no value in discussion of the important, and that becoming rational means setting all deeper convictions of faith aside. This is a not-so-subtle form of hostility, and many students consider it a form of antireligious prejudice. The schools and universities impose secular monism and thereby become as contrary to the true tradition of liberal discourse and democracy as is Rorty's image of the public square. There is a difference: in the public square, secular monists have no power to silence others, whereas in academic institutions they surely do by wielding the power (i.e., the ability to punish) through grading. Even in classes in religious studies, students must set aside their convictions in the interests of impartiality, when they would be better prepared for public life by speaking respectfully as people of faith gathered around a seminar table with equal seating.

The rule of classroom discourse should be civility, respect, logic, tolerance, and an openness to changing one's views, rather than the rule of silence. An agenda of teachers in many universities is to impose the attitude that the voices of believers must be kept quiet unless they are willing to speak without any reference to their beliefs, which are deemed arbitrary and capricious rather than objective. As a university professor, I have seen the many ways in which bias in the form of indifference diminishes the self-esteem of students with religiously based principles who defend these with solid apologetics and reasoning. The hope is that through the educational process these principles will go away and the student will become more objective. This bias is as strong as ever, even though many philosophers acknowledge that there is no perfectly objective "view from nowhere" but only various "views from somewhere" that engage in dialogue. Faculty who do not share this bias toward secular monism, or who are themselves thoughtfully and respectfully religious in some of their own principles, are not likely to gain the full trust of their peers.

In the words of George M. Marsden, all religious perspectives should be welcome in the academy and in the public square "so long as their proponents are willing to support the rules necessary for constructive exchange of ideas in a pluralistic setting."[25] Of course, if some do not firmly adhere to such rules, they are still free to speak, however much one hopes that they will be ignored. Without this pluralistic mix of voices, educational discourse becomes dreary and uniform rather than creative, challenging, and tolerant. The value of democratic pluralistic discourse is that it does not require participants to privatize their core convictions, and this should be modeled in higher education. The context of education is distinguished from politics by pedagogical goals, and therefore rules of respectful discourse should be firmly applied and enforced.

Returning from the sphere of higher education to grade school and high school education, we should not be surprised that parents want their children out of public schools when an atmosphere of indifference dominates. School vouchers become the only way that poor families in inner cities such as Cleveland can free their children from the domain of secular monism and its destructive inculcation. I am pleased that on June 27, 2002, the U.S. Supreme Court, voting 5 to 4, upheld the Cleveland voucher plan, even though nearly all students who receive voucher grants attend religious schools. As Justice William Rehnquist declared, "The Ohio program is entirely neutral with respect to religion. It provides benefits directly to a wide spectrum of individuals, defined only by financial need and residence in a particular school district." No parent is forced to place a child in a religious school, and perhaps no parent would if the public schools created an atmosphere of respect for religious expression and provided chaplains, just as one finds them in the U.S. Congress and in the military. But the assault on religion is so deep that an exodus must be allowed.

Free Spirits in Politics

I am especially chagrined by the view that religion in public life is a "conversation-stopper." On the contrary, it is our most significant conversation starter. On August 28, 1963, Martin Luther King stood before the Lincoln Memorial and spoke of "all God's children" participating in the American dream:

> When we let freedom ring, when we let it ring from every village and every hamlet, from every state and every city, we will be able to speed up that day when all God's children, black men and white men, Jews and Gentiles, Protestants and Catholics, will be able to join hands and sing in the words of that old Negro spiritual, "Free at last! Free at last! Thank God almighty, we are free at last!"[26]

This religious content was not just rhetoric for the sake of emotional engagement. As Richard Neuhaus writes, many public commentators ignored or trivialized the religious conviction underlying King's words and works because "in recent decades we have become accustomed to believe that *of course* America is a secular society. That, in the minds of many, is what is meant by the separation of church and state."[27] When one announcer covering King's memorial service described him as "the son of a minister," he was reflecting the belief that religion "must be kept at one remove from the public square, that matters of *public* significance must be sanitized of religious particularity."[28] Yet Dr. King had remarked, "They aren't interested in the *why* of what we're doing, only in the *what* of what we're doing, and because they don't understand the why they cannot understand the what."[29] The point here is that Dr. King believed in human freedom and justice not merely because these were his values; because these are, as he perceived and felt them, the values and purposes of the Creator of us all, King was willing to speak for them, to act on them, and ultimately to die for them. His entire world of thought and action was based on the notion of *agape* or unlimited love, including the tradition of nonviolent resistance that was passed on to him from his mentors.[30]

The "why" giving rise to the "what" of which King spoke is nicely represented at the international level in the thought and life of Dag Hammarskjöld. Here the relationship between the public servant and the inner religious self is well manifested. When he was killed in a plane crash over Africa in 1961, "the whole world knew that it had lost one of its most dedicated and invaluable public servants."[31] According to Henry P. Van Dusen, Hammarskjöld's leadership as Secretary General transformed the United Nations "from a forum of prolix and often ineffectual talk into an instrument of action by the Community of Nations for the safeguarding of peace and the furtherance of world order."[32] Like Lincoln and King, his religious sensibilities (which were issued in the publication of his spiritual classic entitled *Markings*) and his remarkable political abilities matched exactly the needs of the hour. Hammarskjöld wrote of his religious grounding in all that he did:

> In the faith which is God's marriage to the soul, you are *one* with God, and God is wholly in you, just as, for you, He is wholly in all you meet. With this faith, in prayer you descend into yourself to meet the Other, in the steadfastness and light of this union, alone before God, and each of your acts is an act of creation, conscious because you are a human being with human responsibilities, but governed, nevertheless, by the power beyond human consciousness which has created man.[33]

Hammarskjöld was another of the many truly great public servants who, with tremendous statesmanship born of a desire to be effective for an urgent purpose higher than his own, did so much for so many. His sense of spiritual calling in public life separated him from the despised political opportunist.

In presidential elections these days, public speech often specifically invokes religious values. Senator Joseph Lieberman, for example, as a democratic vice-presidential candidate, often expressed in public speech his core commitment to Judaism. An observant orthodox Jew, he asserted throughout the fall campaign months of 2000 that the nation needed to recover moral standards grounded in spirituality and religion. As a result, critics worried that too much religion was being injected into the political domain. Lieberman was honestly revealing who he was as a candidate, indicating his personal beliefs. There are those who will fear that too much talk of religion in politics will lead eventually to its being coercively legislated, but these fears are both contrary to American tradition and unrealistic in the light of centuries of religious disestablishment. More plausibly, some critics simply did not wish to hear from a politician about his religious beliefs, asserting a nonexistent right to be free from the purported discomfort of allowing others to speak from their hearts. But to speak of one's faith is not to coerce, and to say that such speech burdens the listener is anything but mainstream in a country where nineteen of twenty people say they believe in God, half pray every day, and only 7 percent never pray.[34] When a candidate explains his values and beliefs openly, as George W. Bush commonly does, he is merely being honest, he imposes nothing, and he allows us to know more fully for whom we might be voting.

One hopes that the politicians are not pandering for votes. The fact is that in recent decades many American politicians have failed the nation due to a lack of moral grounding, and as a result, the public seems to welcome the candidate from this rather despised profession who states both his or her moral vision and the religious beliefs, if any, underlying that vision. There are many who would argue that the absence of such speech and vision from the public square has left it devoid of elevated standards, empty of all but the vulgarities of popular culture. People want to know if a politician has a sense of religious calling in entering public life, as did Lincoln, or if he or she is simply an opportunist seeking power, influence, and money. Of course, there is such a thing as inappropriate public religious expression—for example, the injection of religion into narrow legislative agendas, thereby trivializing religion. In such cases, the candidate will presumably suffer the electoral consequences. Yet 65 percent of Americans do believe that religion is key to solving social problems, and 86 percent of African Americans hold this belief.[35]

Ronald F. Thiemann writes that "religious voices should be welcomed into the pluralistic conversation of democracy as long as they agree to abide by the fundamental values of this republic: a commitment to freedom, equality, and mutual respect."[36]

Throughout American history, the religious convictions of the American people have shaped and enhanced social changes. Lincoln brought his religious convictions about human equality directly into his public rhetoric and actions. Rev. King and Rabbi Abraham Joshua Heschel publicly addressed the problem of racism on the basis of Christian and Jewish ethical traditions. Working within the boundaries of respect, pluralism, and respect for the views of others, religious people are an integral part of moral progress in countless areas of public life. As Stephen L. Carter points out in his Massey Lectures at Harvard University, *a pronounced feature of the religious voice is its willingness to be somewhat subversive of the reigning moral and political assumptions of the day in order to achieve progress.*[37] Carter writes:

> Our most famous progressive examples of this subversive aspect of the religions are the abolitionist movement and the civil rights movement, both of which were largely inspired by the shared meanings of religious communities that were sharply different from the meanings that the larger society in those days proposed; both of which changed the nation quite radically for the better; and both of which give the lie to the constitutional canard that there is something wrong, or even something suspicious, about religious argument in American political life.[38]

So while religion should promote civility in public discourse and political debate, *it would be unfortunate if it became too civilized to assert a prophetic voice against the power of injustice.*

Democracy requires a true pluralism. I would find it worthwhile to listen to a white wiccan ("good witch," usually a nature mystic) in the forests of Oregon who has a mystical passion for the environment and nonhuman animals and speaks thoughtfully to her sense of awe before nature. She would interest me at least as much as—and probably more than—a secular utilitarian giving animal welfare speeches on behalf of world vegetarianism. As Kent Greenawalt writes:

> If people must rely on evaluations that are not based on commonly accessible reasons to arrive at positions regarding animal rights and environmental protection, and these positions have important implications for what the law should be, the religious believer has an argument that he should be able to rely on his religiously informed view of humankind's place in the world as he struggles with relevant moral questions and their political and legal implications.[39]

Greenawalt argues, contra Rawls, that there are no absolutely unassailable criteria for public discourse in a liberal democracy. Greenawalt thinks all voices can participate in public debate and discourse, although he recommends these guidelines for all:

> (1) a substantial consensus on the organizing political principles for society; (2) a shared sense that major political discussions will be carried on primarily in secular terms; (3) a respect for religious belief and activity and a hesitancy to attack religious practices as nonsensical; and (4) an assumption that one can be a seriously religious person and a liberal participant in a liberal society.[40]

Because secular moral discourse is inconclusive and thin on many issues, he argues that people must appropriately rely on their religious beliefs and language in public discourse. The free and open expression of religiously grounded moral views was previously considered vital to the health of the nation. Will there be a place in American public life for the Lincolns and Kings of tomorrow? That King made references to the Hebrew prophet Amos when speaking of the concept of justice, rather than speaking in the style of a secular philosopher, only made him that much more politically effective. One wonders why persons whose positions on moral and social issues are grounded in reason informed by religious faith are assumed to be any less capable of civil discourse in the public sphere than say, devoted libertarians, ardent feminists, animal welfarists, deep ecologists, socialists, and so on *ad infinitum*.

In the United States and in western Europe, disputes over the proper place of religious convictions in public life and the extent of religious freedom often include a subtext of fear of theocracy that is directed at Christianity, the dominant Western religion. But after two centuries of success, modern liberal democracies, which are characterized by pluralism, dialogue, and respect for the views of others, are in no realistic danger of reversion to theocracy. With the exception of Calvin's Geneva, the Protectorate in England, and seventeenth-century Massachusetts, where in the Western (or Eastern) Christian world have there been theocracies to revert to?

Civility, Respect, and Tolerance

One of Stephen L. Carter's most useful contributions in the academic conversation about the nature of discourse in the public square is his discussion of civility.[41] He defends the place of religious argument in public debate and of civility in such debate between those who differ. He laments the loss of civility in public debate and politics and sees religion as the key to its reconstruction:

> The key to reconstructing civility, I shall argue, is for all of us to learn anew the virtue of acting with love toward our neighbors. Love of neighbor has long been a tenet of Judaism and Christianity, and a revival of civility in America

will require a revival of all that is best in religion as a force in our public life. Only religion possesses the majesty, the power, and the sacred language to teach all of us, the religious and the secular, the genuine appreciation for each other on which a successful civility must rest.[42]

His general argument is that secularists have *not* done well over the last decade in creating an atmosphere of political civility and that any hope for a rebirth of civility will begin with the purposeful commitment of religious participants to the principle of neighbor love. This is the hope for civility in the world of Walzer's authentic democratic debate, rather than the tomes of Rorty and Rawls. After all, open democratic discourse in Western politics developed in the United States out of the Congregationalist tradition and from the left wing of the English Puritan Reformation.[43] Jane Mansbridge, a leading communitarian political philosopher, points out that the very possibility of restoring a "nonadversarial" form of democratic dialogue that avoids the acrimony and intolerance of today's discourse rests with a recovery of something akin to the New England town meetings of the seventeenth and eighteenth centuries, where the ethos of mutual respect was grounded in religious tradition.[44]

People with religious convictions will often be less zealous and more respectful of the opinions of others than many representatives from secular social movements. There are many erudite political leaders with deep religion-based moral principles who do not overuse religious language in debates over public policy. If the religious voice is to be taken at all seriously, it should not address the trivial issues of the day. There is nothing more likely to fall on deaf ears than the voice of the aggressive political-religious zealot who claims to have the direct word of the Supreme Being on everything and anything.

Yet it would be unrealistic to hope that the moral weight of religious traditions will be publicly invoked only when the tradition itself represents a clear consensus view on this issue. Indeed, religious traditions have been divided on major issues such as slavery, capital punishment, just war, economic and social justice, and the integrity of marriage as foundation for family building.[45] Sometimes waiting for consensus will not suffice the conscientious citizen and believer.

Religious communities often need to do more to educate their own members about certain moral insights and assume that they will have a ripple effect on the surrounding culture. The Moral Majority of the 1970s and 1980s was triumphalist in tone, often unwilling to engage in serious and respectful dialogue with those of differing viewpoints. It was too exclusively committed to cultural change through political elections, as opposed to effective social reform movements in the spirit of the great benevolent associations of the nineteenth century. The success of Chuck Colson with Prison Fellowship is a respected example of such reform.[46]

There is little doubt that the strong secular liberal movement to deny political expression to persons of religious conscience (in particular, those of a more conservative conscience) stems in some part from the excesses of some religious voices. The secular movement itself, however, is wrong and in theoretical violation of religious free exercise. In a democracy, everyone has the right to engage in the political process on religious or secular terms; a person's success or failure will depend on the quality of his or her moral positions and conduct.

There are moments when the religious person must speak from a religious perspective to address a high-stakes public issue. These moments should be carefully chosen if this voice is to be taken seriously. Precisely the same caution should be taken by feminists, deconstructionists, African Americans, Marxists, social conservatives, and many others who have meaningful voices in a pluralistic and liberal polity that deserve to be heard. Although background worldviews and epistemic priorities may vary, a liberal polity enables those different voices that happen to agree practically to create alliances. Any voice that lacks intellectual rigor and that displays imperialistic arrogance, incivility in discourse, or lack of attentive listening to other voices should ultimately have no impact—although one cannot be certain that in some cases it won't.

Critics of the religious voice insist on the single language of secular monism in addressing matters of the commonweal. While many issues can be addressed by the believer in the purely secular rational language necessary for public policy, they need not be, and there are times when the specifically religious language of the believer is the only language game that can make the necessary point. Surely, both Protestants and Catholics should have spoken out against Nazism from their theological traditions much earlier than they did; Dietrich Bonhoeffer was an eloquent exception whose voice was silenced only by death in a Nazi prison. Often the religious voice plays a constructive role without which public dialogue would be impoverished. However, this voice is not needed in trivial or less urgent matters unrelated to the essential dignity of human persons.

Those who wish to curtail freedom of religious expression in the public sphere work hard to establish the most negative stereotypes of the religious voice as uncivil. Gilles Kepel's 1991 book entitled *La Revanche de Dieu* (The Revenge of God), for example, harped on the Ayatollah Khomeini in Iran and militant Zionists of the Gush Emunin in Israel. His book was a bestseller in France.[47] He threw the American Protestant Moral Majority in with these other groups as if there were no discontinuities. For Kepel, it would be ideal if religious belief would disappear from public life as a result of the eroding force of secularization, but this does not seem to be happening in most parts of the world.

An alternative and fairer perspective is provided by José Casanova, a sociologist of religion who clarifies the emergence of "public religions in the modern world."[48] Casanova demonstrates how religious traditions in the West have long played a successful role in public discourse consistent with the rules of respect and pluralism, having long ago abandoned as deeply flawed the notion of religious authoritarianism and state control.

Thiemann summarizes the historic meaning of the free exercise of religion in the American Republic around the values of liberty, equality, and toleration. "All expressions of religion genuinely grounded in conscience are to be tolerated, and no expression is to be proscribed or coerced by an external agency. In particular, since religious exercise is grounded in divine obligation, the claims of civil society on the believer's conscience must always be limited."[49] After taking the draconian arguments of the secular monists to task, Thiemann nicely describes "the pluralist citizen and conditions of publicity." He writes:

> In a pluralistic democracy in which freedom of speech is guaranteed, it is a mistake, I believe, to define any "threshold requirements" that political arguments must meet in order to enter the political debate. Rather, we should seek to define those virtues of citizenship that we seek to instill in all participants in our pluralistic democracy.[50]

Thiemann indicates a series of norms that define such virtuous citizenship. The first is reliance on noncoercive means of building consensus through a process of dialogue that will "inevitably assign high value to the broad accessibility of public arguments."[51] While such broad accessibility of arguments can be encouraged and is strategically useful in consensus building, it "cannot, however, be *demanded* in a society that protects free speech as a fundamental right."[52] The second norm is mutual respect, including "the recognition that these are morally defensible alternatives to one's own point of view" that others may hold with genuine conviction.[53] Third is the norm of moral integrity, which includes consistency of speech and principle. Any behavior that denies the moral integrity of one's opponents and any words that dehumanize them are unacceptable, even when it comes to important issues. Thiemann gives the example of King's nonviolent civility when confronted by racists.[54] He concludes that "there is no fundamental incompatibility between public religious arguments and the essential conditions of publicity in a pluralistic democracy."[55] While public arguments that are inaccessible, disrespectful, or lacking in moral integrity cannot be banned, they should be resisted.

"The genius of America," concludes Thiemann, "is that it did not require persons to abandon their ethnic identity as the price of citizenship."[56] The politics of the particular does not threaten democracy, and the presence of "stridency and passion may be signs of the robustness of democracy rather than indications of its decay."[57] Multiculturalism and multireligionism enhance our democracy.

In addition to laying out the above norms, Thiemann debunks these two myths:

(1) "Religious belief is inherently irrational or nonrational; therefore religious warrants can never meet appropriate standards of publicity."[58]

(2) "Religious beliefs, particularly those that make claims to truth, are not compatible with democracy's fundamental value of tolerance or mutual respect and should therefore be prohibited from the public realm."[59]

Some critics of religious expression argue that religious voices are too shrill. Although there may be some shrill voices, both religious and secular, that lack the statesmanship and civility to be taken very seriously in public discourse, the shrillness of a voice itself does not preclude it from public dialogue. The abolitionists were certainly shrill (so were the Muckrakers), and they would say of necessity and with good reason. The point is that they believed that shrillness was necessary to make themselves heard when the other side deliberately and systematically silenced them. Frustration, as well as self-righteousness, can bring out shrillness, and sometimes a bit of this is both creative and called for in genuinely multicultural discourse.

No one who is seriously committed to multiculturalism and the democratic way can overlook the positive role of spiritual and religious values in shaping civic virtue and emphasizing responsibility in proportion to freedom; most people get their moral values from religion, and moral values are the underpinnings of democratic freedom. Nor could anyone committed to democracy and the American way wish for a public world where religious expression is driven away into the sphere of purely private life. Desmond Tutu, the prophet of justice; Gandhi, the practitioner of nonviolence; Eugene Rivers of Boston, who brought an end to inner-city gang violence; and Hammarskjöld, seeker of peace in the Congo: all are examples of modern leaders whose deep religious convictions shaped their contributions to public life, political change, and human progress. They manifested superb diplomatic courtesy in order to accomplish unquestionably laudable public goals, yet none could be accused of the form of "politeness" that does not dare to speak out over social convention as others suffer. They were people who thought for themselves with courage and caring, in a manner informed by intelligent faith. Such persons understood the rules of liberal democratic pluralism. They compelled no one, except with the power of their love, service, and sacrifice. Some died for their causes, following the historic pattern of Lincoln, another profoundly and explicitly religious thinker and public speaker who inspired a nation.[60] Would anyone wish to keep such leading public lights in the dark? Some would, certainly, but not for good or right reasons.

Rather than undermining human freedom and civility, the religious impulse has often served as the very groundwork for its enhancement. There are, indeed, compelling arguments as to the central role of Judaism and Christianity in providing the matrix for democratic pluralism and open political society that deserve mention as this chapter concludes.

"Positive Neutrality"

We live in a time when rude, vulgar, and obscene public expression has achieved remarkable new heights in song and media, in schools and politics, in parks and village squares, in the workplace and in the sports arena. Nothing is unspeakable or hidden, no matter how much it imposes on decency. Everyone and everybody is out of the closet, public and free about who and what they are in an era of every sort of liberation from restraint. Yet the public display of a religious symbol, the wearing of a religious garb, the simple act of public prayer, and the public articulation of the connection between spiritual and ethical/political values are considered by some to be the one area where liberty must not spread.

The aggressive effort to enforce a secular humanist view of the universe and of human nature has serious defenders. One legal scholar, for example, argued that the establishment clause of the First Amendment calls for "the banishment of religion from the public square," as well as all public places, ceremonies, and discourse.[61] Better informed scholars, with a sense of the place of religious freedom in American history and in the minds of the founders, have pointed out that the establishment clause does not imply the hegemony of secularism.[62]

In the final analysis, freedom of religious expression in public domains is a test case for the very existence of a true democracy. I cite Neuhaus:

> The question of religion's access to the public square is not first of all a question of First Amendment law. It is first of all a question of understanding the theory and practice of democratic governance. Citizens are the bearers of opinion, including opinion shaped by or espousing religious belief, and citizens have equal access to the public square. In this representative democracy, the state is forbidden to determine which convictions and moral judgments may be proposed for public deliberation. Through a constitutionally ordered process, the people will deliberate and the people will decide.[63]

In other words, our attention should always be on the rights of a citizen in our democracy to speak without being censored.

In addition, such freedom of expression is a matter of First Amendment rights. As A. James Reichley indicates in his masterful overview, "Since the 1940s the Court has sometimes seemed to interpret prohibition of establishment to mean not only that there should be no direct tie between government and the organized churches but also that the whole of civil society should be kept insulated against contact with religion."[64] Yet freedom of religion absolutely requires that human beings be allowed to express themselves as they wish in public. Regrettably, as Stephen V. Monsma concludes,

> The bottom line is that the Supreme Court's decisions are supportive of a secularized public sphere that is not neutral on religion and nonreligion. Those who seek to live

out a religious faith in all walks of their lives (in the education of their children, in the public policies they advocate, and in the acts of charity and social responsibility they take) face insistent direct and indirect hindrances and discouragement.[65]

Monsma argues that the courts have tended to enforce a secular public culture. Many courts have tended to deny the right of persons of various religious traditions to display their symbols in public places and have at times stated that religion should be excluded from politics. These tendencies, argues Monsma, amount to an abandonment of neutrality between secularism and religion and result in discrimination against the latter.[66]

Others are interpreting the American scenario in terms similar to Monsma's. John Witte, for example, after an extensive and detailed overview of Supreme Court cases, concludes that the Court has effectively established secularism against religions, allowing the suppression of anything but the secular viewpoint. Witte underscores that this extreme departure from historical precedent underlies much of the resentment that religious people express when speaking of government. He argues conclusively that the Constitution, by all coherent interpretation, was intended to encourage pluralism rather than suppress it:

> One theme common to these cases, however, is that public religion must be as free as private religion. Not because the religious groups in these cases are really nonreligious. Not because their public activities are really nonsectarian. And not because their public expressions are really part of the cultural mainstream. To the contrary, these public groups and activities deserve to be free just because they are religious, just because they engage in sectarian practices, just

because they sometimes take stands above, beyond, and against the mainstream. They provide leaven and leverage for the polity to improve.[67]

As Witte shows, the free exercise clause forbids

> proscriptions of religion—actions that unduly burdened conscience, restricted religious expression, discriminated against religion, or invaded the autonomy of churches and other religious bodies. The disestablishment clause outlawed government prescriptions of religion—actions that coerced the conscience, mandated forms of religious expression, discriminated in favor of religion, or improperly allied the state with churches or other religious bodies.[68]

In essence, then, "both the free exercise and the disestablishment clauses thereby provided complementary protections to the first principles of the American experiment—liberty of conscience, freedom of religious expression, equality of plural faiths before the law, and separation of church and state."[69]

As Phillip E. Hammond argues, "The Founders recognized that the Puritan rendition of a just society was but one of many such renditions, and subsequent interpreters of their constitutional handiwork have broadened that recognition. But it does not follow that the result is a nonreligious viewpoint."[70] The protection of conscience is too valuable for the hegemony of any particular secular or religious anthropology. It is not religion itself that must be pushed into the underground; rather, as Hammond writes, it is "the *authority* of religion, its capacity to give orders on its own terms in public."[71] "Does the modern 'public square' require that the church stay out? Most assuredly not," concludes Hammond.[72]

Monsma's solution to the problem of enforced silence on religious expression is one with which I concur. He calls it "positive neutrality" and defines it as follows: "Under positive neutrality, government is *neutral* in that it does not recognize or favor any one religion or religious group over any other, nor does it favor or recognize religious groups or religion as a whole over secular groups or secular philosophies and mind-sets as a whole."[73] Monsma defines the first feature of positive neutrality thus:

> The first feature of pluralism's mind-set regarding religion and society is its perception that it is natural, healthy, and proper for the people of the United States to adhere to a great variety of faith communities and to join a wide range of churches and other religious associations, and for some to adhere to no religious faith at all. This is seen as the appropriate consequence of a free society. Structural pluralism welcomes religion in its various manifestations and in its various activities as a legitimate, contributing, integral part of U.S. society, including its political aspects. Not merely religion-in-general but also particularistic religion, whose adherents take it as an authoritative force in their lives, is respected and accepted as a part of the life of the U.S. polity.[74]

Persons of no religious faith or persuasion should be as respected and free in their expression as are their religious fellow citizens. Furthermore, just as the state provides funding to support programs and projects of public benefit to society through secular institutions and structures, so also should it do so for such programs sponsored by the various religious groups so long as resources go to directly benefit the this-worldly aspects of the common good, rather than to prayer books or other religious items.[75] However, the religious symbols and artifacts that naturally exist within the grounds of a church or mosque, for example, should be left to stand as testimony to the value of faith-based programs. Support for faith-based social programs, as affirmed by the Clinton-Gore administration and then more emphatically by the Bush administration, is the only approach consistent with nondiscrimination. (Some religious groups may prefer to avoid such public support without gaining exemptions from certain laws and regulations that contradict their teachings.)

A further image of life under positive neutrality might be a new form of daily legislative prayer that reflects true pluralism, as Monsma describes. Instead of vague generalities, such prayer should reflect the pluralism of the American people that government serves:

> The state would maintain its neutrality by inviting a rotating schedule of representatives of a wide variety of religious associations and faith communities, each of whom would be encouraged to offer a prayer within his or her religious tradition. One day a Fundamentalist Protestant would open the session with prayer; the next, a Unitarian; the next, a Catholic priest; the next, a Mormon; the next, a mainline Protestant; the next, a Jewish rabbi; and so on. Confirmed secularists should also be asked to take their turn by opening the daily session with a moment of quiet reflection on the importance of the tasks lying ahead that day or in some other appropriate manner.[76]

This true neutrality between religions and between religion and nonreligion is appropriate, I would add, for public schools, for public holiday celebrations and displays, and the like. Only those groups, either religious or secular, that clearly espouse hate and maleficence should be excluded.

An account by Frederick Mark Gedicks concluded, "While the majority of Americans support the general principle of separation of church and state, most strongly disagree with the strictness and vigor with which the Supreme Court has located and policed the boundary."[77] One hopes for a less hostile Court that will shape future decisions less antagonistic to religious expression. On July 15, 1999, the United States House of Representatives voted 306 to 118 to pass a bill meant to protect religious practices from government interference. Powerful testimony in Congress included accounts of prisoners barred from receiving communion, students disciplined in public schools for wearing yarmulkes, congregations being denied the right to build places of worship in residential areas, Muslim firefighters being forced to shave their beards, Hmong corpses being submitted for autopsy even though relatives believe this condemns their spirits eternally, and Roman Catholic priests being prohibited from serving communion wine to minors. Yet the act in its final rendition addresses issues of religious organizations and land ownership for the most part and is so weakened that it can only be viewed as being of very limited value.

There are really two competing views of the human being underlying the debate about public life and religious expression. In one, the human being is seen as having a built-in religious drive and a desire to express this aspect of humanity. In the other, the human being is seen as not "really" having this religious interest. These two views of the human are in conflict. *The state cannot allow the dominance of the secular view.* If the state takes up secular orthodoxy, it will result in the invalidation and marginalization of religious persons. The state need not promote religion. It must, however, deem the religious drive as worthy of serious protection and avoid secular hegemony.

A Sermonic Conclusion

The secular monists often assume that the religious voice is ultimately a threat to freedom and liberal democracy, and this is one reason why they are so unwilling to let it cross the threshold. Insofar as this is an essay and therefore allows a moment of rhetorical flourish, I wish to correct the above misconception.

It is interesting that religion is sometimes understood to be more contrary to the spirit of freedom than is the case. Historically, religious freedom gave rise to all others. There are, of course, alternative candidates. James Q. Wilson, for example, traces the flowering of individual expression to the emergence of consensual marriage in Western history. Here the individual was finally freed from the stifling nature of marriages that were arranged and enforced by parents and clans, thereby allowing for a free emotional expression of consent or dissent.[78] Wilson argues that this area of consent gave rise to the flowering of individuality that would inevitably spill over into other spheres of human experience, from literature and the arts to politics and economics. Wilson forgets, however, that the emergence of consensual marriage in the thirteenth century was due entirely to the spiritual authority of the church against the hegemony of the clans.[79]

The first chapter of Genesis discloses a God who exists prior to the sun, moon, stars, and all living things. It uses religious language to establish the political-theological point of monotheism, as well as something like an anthropic principle. All the things and persons of this world are absolutely dependent upon God for being and meaning. This dependence never ceases; they are not themselves divine. The sun, the moon, and the stars are not gods to be worshiped; neither are fish or other living creatures meant to be gods. All are part of the anthropic generativity, behind which lies a Creative Presence. Kings and pharaohs, who were seen as gods or sons of gods and worshiped as such by servile masses, are nothing more than the anthropic results of the true Creative Presence, who as such ontologically rules out the worship of such half-gods. The idolatrous worship of political rulers and of the state was once and for all rejected by the Jews. A Creative Presence de-divinizes rulers and thus limits their authority over conscience. The Egyptians identified the pharaoh with the god Horus or with the sun god Ra. These "human divinities" ruled from on high; they alone were free, while all others were their slaves. Amenhotep IV tried to de-divinize the pharaohs by introducing the worship of Aten, the Creator God of monotheism. There was great opposition because it was thought that pharaohs would lose their absolute power. After Amenhotep's death, pharaoh worship resumed. Where Amenhotep failed, the Jews succeeded. Thus, when the Syrian despot Antiochus IV "Epiphanes" (or "manifestation of the divine") attempted to force the Jews to worship him in the second century B.C.E., they revolted. Similarly, the Jews resisted the Roman Emperor Augustus, who proclaimed himself "divine savior." To worship anyone less than God (Yahweh) runs afoul of all that Judaism means. Yahweh did more for the cause of human freedom in Western culture than most secular humanists realize. There is the old African American spiritual: "Oh, let us all from bondage flee, let my people go; and let us all in Christ be free, let my people go."

When the free expression of religious belief in a Creative Presence is inhibited, it has historically been replaced by other beliefs, such as the Nordic myth of Aryan superiority and the ritual of Hitler worship; the anomie of the Sartrean; the complete cultural obsession with the tonality of the body, the filling of the "soul" with the hedonic; and the passion for violence that gives rise to school killing sprees. Of course, religion itself must be viewed with ambivalence, for it will generally tap the benevolent aspects of human nature, but misused it can tap hateful tendencies.

It is important to underscore the fact that religious freedom's ripple effect into other essential freedoms has not only been a matter of the individual conscience beholden to a power higher than the state. There has been a necessary and democratically beneficial presence of religious institutions that have, as organized communities of faith, resisted the totalitarian ambitions of the state. According to T. M. Parker, in his classic Bampton Lectures at Oxford, the distinction between church and state has been a significant force for the rise of freedom in Western civilization. While, realistically, the idea of theocracy has perished from the world, there is the modern problematic of the church's "survival in the face of a State with ever-increasing claims and ambitions—until at last the Leviathan collapses under his own weight."[80] Neuhaus rightly emphasizes that religious freedom is grounded in the tension between the individual and the state and between religious institutions and the state:

> That is, once religion is reduced to nothing more than privatized conscience, the public square has only two actors in it—the state and the individual. Religion as a mediating structure—a community that generates and transmits moral values—is no longer available as a countervailing force to the ambitions of the state. Whether in Hitler's Third Reich or in today's sundry states professing Marxist-Leninism, the chief attack is not upon individual religious belief. Individual religious belief can be dismissed scornfully as superstition, for it finally poses little threat to the power of the state. No, the chief attack is upon the *institutions* that bear and promulgate belief in a transcendent reality by which the state can be called to judgment. Such institutions threaten the totalitarian proposition that everything is to be within the state, nothing is to be outside the state.[81]

The dualism of religious community and state offers the necessary alternative to the state monism that, as John Courtney Murray argued, leads inevitably to absolutism. For the state will surely rush to fill the moral and religious void with its own ambitions. To quote Neuhaus, "conceptually there is no alternative to a *de facto* state religion once traditional religion is driven from the public square."[82] While I have emphasized the individual's impulse toward a Supreme Being throughout this book, I do not wish to lose sight of the role of communities and institutions. In support of *Homo religiosus*, such institutions have pushed back the total moral, spiritual, familial, and social authority of the ancient divine ruler. Lord Acton summarized Anglo-American history a hundred years ago by writing, "The idea that religious liberty is the generating principle of civil, and that civil liberty is the necessary condition of religious, was a discovery reserved for the seventeenth century."[83] Or, in the words of William Temple, "Freedom here—as in Holland— has its origin chiefly in the claim of Dissenters from the established Church to worship God as their consciences might direct. It was rooted in faith."[84] It is a cadre of leading political philosophers who wish to banish the religious voice from the public square that set the stage for new monisms and absolutisms should anyone give them much heed. Fortunately, the real world of politics has passed them by.

An Appeal to Liberty, Human Nature, the American Experiment, and Peaceful Acculturation

In this brief conclusion, I wish to reiterate four related reasons for recognizing the value of freedom of religious expression in public domains, the second of which has been primary in this essay, although all four have received attention.

First, there is the appeal to freedom itself. Those who sense nothing of a Creative Presence, or who for reasons of personal history resent all things religious, should be democratically minded enough to acknowledge the freedom of others to believe and to express their beliefs. A principle of liberal democracy is that such freedom of expression is an inalienable right untrumped by the idiosyncratic sense of annoyance that some have in even catching a glimpse of religious expression in the world around them. Surely such hypersensitivity is unreasonable and should not be indulged by any institutions that claim to be genuinely public, whether schools, courts, or the public square.

It is too much to expect those who sense nothing of a Creative Presence to accept the plausible idea that the inclination toward God is an essential aspect of the "normality of human functioning," as Jacques Maritain defines natural law, although such an inclination is nearly ubiquitous in the past as well as the present.[1] But we can expect from such individuals a recognition of the "negative right" of noninterference with respect to religious and other forms of expression that are neither malicious or indecent. They might also appreciate the value of enhanced mutual understanding that such expression makes possible. Imagine the possibility of delight in having some greater understanding of how people of different religious traditions view the world.

Second, there is the appeal to the objective ontological structure of human nature. Resting the right to public religious expression on the idea of noninterference and freedom, while adequate, relinquishes and ignores a whole set of objective claims about human nature and essential inclinations that the classical natural tradition affirms. The distinguished legal scholar John T. Noonan has written a statement representative of the Anglican and Catholic natural law tradition highlighting the objective nature of the religious inclination: "That religion has caused many acts of violence and perpetuated many hatreds is a datum of history. So has sex. Humankind cannot do without sex; sex cannot be eliminated in order to eliminate its attendant evils."[2] Relegating the religious inclination to the sphere of purely subjective meaning, as if it had no higher objective status than the whimsical creations of the imagination, is a severe diminishment of its significance and power. The fact of the matter is that human beings, from the dawn of history and with relatively few exceptions, have an urge for the transcendent, by which I mean an orientation to some presence in the universe higher than their own that creates for them a mysterious destiny and purpose beyond the limits of time and space.

Third, there is the appeal to the time-honored wisdom of the American experiment. The relative ubiquity of this inclination has been time-honored by the various symbols and ceremonial references to God that the founders of the Republic saw fit to include in various public features of the American experiment. They did not overdo this, and it is in some respects salutary that while the Declaration of Independence refers to God, the Constitution does not. But here and there are phrases and symbols, such as "In God We Trust," which give minimal acknowledgment to the religious inclination; these leave the definition of God wide open to the myriad of interpretations both natural and supernatural, from "ultimate concern" to "unlimited love." Such an acknowledgment is wise because it provides the vague symbolic context to which a highly pluralistic nation, when broken by "limit situations," whether this be an external attack or an internal conflict such as the Civil War, can appeal. The founders of the Republic seem to have understood this dynamic of human nature, and they made allowances for it as they engaged in the revolutionary struggles for freedom. They acknowledged a place for spirituality and religion without wanting to establish any kind of state church.

Not only did they moderately acknowledge this human inclination in the ceremonial and symbolic context, but as they asserted the prohibition against the establishment of any state religion they simultaneously refused to "prohibit the free exercise" of religion. This fundamental right against the censoring of religious expression in public and private life is perhaps the single greatest accomplishment of the American experiment in liberty, and it is something about which we should all be especially proud. Just because this accomplishment is now more than two centuries old does not make it any less meaningful.

Thus, a decent respect for liberal freedoms, for human nature, and for the genius of the founders requires nothing less than the fullest liberty of religious expression across public domains, limited only by the principle of nonmaleficence. This expression is not objectionable, nor does it require any apologetics before the annoyed and resentful atheist who is engaged in "fostering atheism as the non-faith of the nation."[3] I have argued that underlying such engagement, whether in the schools or the public square, is a set of anthropological assertions about human nature that, in a post-Marxist and post-Freudian era, must fall under the rubric of secular existentialism. And I have associated secular existentialism with malaise and lack of higher purpose.

Fourth and finally, there is the appeal to peaceful acculturation. For those who wish to thrust their neighbor's religious expression and reason for living into the realm of forced public silence, out of sight and out of mind, the current reality of various nodes of world conflict that are agitated by religious differences affords a handy point of reference. It is undeniable that religion can tap these negative aspects of human nature and sustain horrific conflict, although it must be said that, on the whole, religion has no worse record than secular ideologies, and probably a better one. The secular ideologies of the twentieth century, such as Nazism and Marxist-Leninism, brought systematic hatred and genocide to new levels. Because religion is supposed to be a force for good, we are especially critical of it when it fails. Noonan writes in stark terms:

> Of all the violences and hatreds of humankind, that based on religion has been the most injurious, not because of the intensity of feeling and ferocity of execution that it has engendered—mere political ideologies have done greater damage in these respects—but because of the harm it has done religion itself, mocking its mandates, denying its duties, perverting its purpose. None, I dare declare, is more hateful to God.[4]

Noonan sees the solution to this problem in the uniquely American invention of freedom of religion, although he does not choose to explain this.

His meaning, I think, is reasonably implicit. But allow me to be more explicit: where religion shows its dark side through opposition to good science, conflicts such as "holy wars," and impassioned arrogance, the best solution ever devised by humanity is freedom of religious expression, which subjects believers to the corrective pressures of public response and exposes them to more enlightened alternative worldviews. This has been the historical view of even those liberals who themselves have no interest in religion other than to see that its negative potential is kept under control.[5] By enforcing privatization in the schools and in the public square, we further isolate some potentially quite regressive subcultures, leaving them to fester in their ignorance and misunderstanding of others until wanton violence explodes. It would be better to expose fanaticisms of any kind, religious or secular, to the process of learning to live peacefully with persons of all beliefs. Violent potentialities are gradually eroded by the observation that people of various traditions can live side by side in respect, reconciliation, and freedom.

A purpose of America is to provide the entire world with a model of how people of all faiths, including secularism, can freely express their core values in civil and respectful discourse, thereby enhancing mutual understanding and appreciation amid continuities without denying difference. The censoring of the religious voice under the terms of secular monism, whether in schools or in the public square, entirely violates this creative purpose.

Let us return to the second appeal, which is so central to this essay. Noonan takes a position on human nature with which I am in agreement. If religion is merely a projection of human personal and collective need, then religious freedom is afforded "no secure footing."[6] While Noonan acknowledges that religion is in part projection, he holds that "religion is also a response to another, an other who is not a human being, an other who must have an intelligence and a will and so be, analogously, a person. . . . Religion is ineradicable because of this other and greater to whom we relate and respond."[7] Noonan is claiming, then, that the secure footing for religious freedom rests in the reality of relationship between the human creature and God. The reality of this relationship is something that Noonan cannot prove, and he has no interest in integrating his metaphysical claims with scientific reflection on the human religious inclination and its origins. But he is correct in making the observation that this inclination is as permanent a feature of human experience as is sex. It is this inclination that, more than any other, is responsible for the historical emergence of freedom, for it links the human being with two levels of reality, one of which, the supernatural, takes precedence over the natural and thereby strips all earthly powers of any ultimacy.[8]

The religious inclination will not go away, nor should it, because it is essential rather than peripheral to who and what we as human creatures are. This assertion is at the very heart of the Catholic and Anglican natural law tradition and is clearly a subtext in efforts to add objective scientific credibility to the perennial idea that the reconciliation between humankind and God is the purpose underlying the universe.

Like Noonan, I do not wish to compartmentalize religion as a purely subjective conferring of a sense of purpose in the universe. Like Teilhard de Chardin, I wish to assert the radical improbability of a line of development from the "stuff of the universe" to "the birth of thought" and the awareness of a "Great Presence."[9] Chardin conceived of this Presence not "up there," but as "up ahead," drawing the universe into the future toward unity. "A universal love," he argued, "is not only psychologically possible; it is the only complete and final way in which we are able to love."[10]

What is at stake, of course, is an elevation of the groundwork of religious freedom from the still important sphere of purely subjective meaning and autonomy to a more objective claim about evolved human nature. Insofar as the human religious inclination plausibly points toward an objective referent, the whole field of religion and science becomes relevant. I disagree with Steven Goldberg, who warns paternalistically against trying to find evidence of "spirituality" in the physical universe. He claims that science and religion constitute different realms of human thought. His concern is with the shifting sands of scientific discovery that may substantiate religious beliefs today but undermine them tomorrow.[11] Such a warning is well intentioned. It does seem, however, that the universe, nature, and human nature do raise religious questions that can be responded to empirically. An enormous amount of serious writing since the early 1990s suggests that dialogue between science and religion is of fundamental importance.[12] The modern effort to take science seriously as a natural theological perspective has roots that reach back to earlier decades in writings that are often well worth reviewing.

The atheist feels that he or she is alone in the universe, and he or she should be respected for such views, although not specially indulged. Insofar as the atheist presses to remove all the trappings of "ceremonial deism" from public rituals and presses aggressively for a censoring of fellow citizens in public domains, he or she must be repudiated in the name of freedom, nature, and tradition. It is noteworthy that such defiant atheists depart from the Enlightenment deism around which the Republic was formed. The Enlightenment deists viewed the existence of God as self-evident and the religious propensity as innate.[13] There were a very few who were not of this opinion, but they did not win the day then, and they should not do so today.

If the entire course of history is evidence, it appears that the denial of a Creative Presence is difficult to live "down to the very roots of the human will," using another phrase from Jacques

Maritain.[14] This is indicated by the fact that whenever atheism has been imposed by the state, as was the case in the secular totalitarianisms of the twentieth century, it has failed. *Homo religiosus* has evolutionary roots too deep to be repressed for long, despite the concerted use of secular coercion. A true humanism can only be one that celebrates all the evolved and coevolved capacities for good that have come to define human nature as we have responded to all that is present in the universe. The forms of thought, ritual, and belief that, however diverse, find a unifying principle in a Creative Presence in the universe that is higher than our own are as numerous as the stars in the heavens. It is from this sense of a Creative Presence that an impression of our common humanity has emerged in human consciousness to form the center of ethical and moral life. We can no longer proceed into the future without taking into account the human longing for God—both in ourselves and in our misguided enemies—that prior to the modern era was taken to be absolutely "natural to the human creature."[15]

I have tried to update the case for *Homo religiosus,* drawing on some scientific perspectives and studies to support what is a commonplace observation. It is on some level almost silly to marshal scientific studies to substantiate that which is perfectly obvious. We do not need science to tell us that we are generally a religious species. In various ways throughout the essay, I have applied this image of human nature to problems of freedom of expression in public domains, chiefly in public education and in politics. These two domains are in various ways connected, for the strict privatization of religion in the schools is preparatory for continued privatization in political and ethical discourse. In essence, the forced privatization of spiritual and religious expression assigns to an important and beneficial human capacity a molelike status, below the surface and in the dark.

A true liberal democracy—the one the founders of the American Republic established—must give the religious and the secular citizen equal seating with regard to public expression across all domains, including education, on the grounds of respect for autonomy alone, but also on the grounds that the spiritual-religious image of human nature is at least as plausible as the secular image and possibly more so.

Ecclesiastes tells us that there is "nothing new under the sun." There is nothing new in this essay. Sometimes we take old truths for granted, so much so that they become uninteresting and we begin to forget them. Thus the need for the occasional reminder. Or perhaps we doubt them because they are not substantiated for the modern scientific temper. I will have succeeded if I have, in an interesting way, rearticulated the old.

Notes

Notes to Introduction

1. Pascal Boyer, *Religion Explained* (New York: Basic Books, 2001).

2. Andrew Newberg, Eugene G. d'Aquili, and Vince Rause, *Why God Won't Go Away: Brain Science and the Biology of Belief* (New York: Ballantine Books, 2001).

3. David Sloan Wilson, *Darwin's Cathedral: Evolution, Religion, and the Nature of Society* (Chicago: University of Chicago Press, 2002).

4. Harold G. Koenig, Michael E. McCullough, and David B. Larson, eds., *Handbook of Religion and Health* (New York: Oxford University Press, 2001).

5. See John Courtney Murray, S. J., *We Hold These Truths: Catholic Reflections on the American Proposition* (New York: Sheed and Ward, 1960).

6. See Daniel A. Dombrowski, "Tradition and Religion: The Case of Stephen R. L. Clark," *Sophia* 36, no. 1 (1997): 96–123.

7. Julian Huxley, *Religion without Revelation* (New York: New American Library, 1957), p. 191.

8. Ibid., p. 194.

9. Huston Smith, *Why Religion Matters: The Fate of the Human Spirit in an Age of Disbelief* (San Francisco: HarperSanFrancisco, 2001), p. 11.

10. Ibid., p. 34.

11. Ibid., p. 35.

12. Ibid., p. 45.

13. Ibid., p. 49.

14. Robert Wright, *Nonzero: The Logic of Human Destiny* (New York: Vintage Books, 2000), p. 8.

15. Paul Davies, *The Mind of God: The Scientific Basis for a Rational World* (New York: Simon and Schuster, 1993), p. 20.

16. Ibid., p. 232.

17. Paul Davies, *The Fifth Miracle: The Search for the Origin and Meaning of Life* (New York: Simon and Schuster, 2000), p. 273.

18. Paul Davies, *Other Worlds: Space, Superspace and the Quantum Universe* (London: Penguin Books, 1990), p. 161.

19. For other distinguished scientists' views, see See Russell Stannard, *The God Experiment: Can Science Prove the Existence of God?* (London: Faber and Faber, 1999); and John Polkinghorne, *Faith, Science and Understanding* (New Haven, Conn.: Yale University Press, 2000).

20. Augustine, *Confessions,* book 1, 1.

21. See John Tyers, foreword to *Worship,* by Evelyn Underhill (1936; reprint, Guilford, England: Eagle Press, 1991); Kenneth Stevenson, introduction to Underhill, *Worship.*

22. R. R. Marett, *Sacraments of Simple Folk* (Oxford: Clarendon Press, 1932).

23. See Steven Mithen, *The Prehistory of the Mind: A Search for the Origins of Art, Religion and Science* (London: Thames and Hudson, 1996).

24. John Hick, *The Fifth Dimension: An Exploration of the Spiritual Realm* (Oxford: Oneworld Publications, 1999), p. 3.

25. Good News Club v Milford Central School, June 11, 2001, No. 99–2036.

26. See "Top Court Gives Religious Clubs Equal Footing in Grade Schools," *New York Times,* June 12, 2001, A1, A22.

27. Beth McMurtrie, "Pluralism and Prayer under One Roof: College Revamps Chapels and Programs to Serve a More Diverse Group of Students," *Chronicle of Higher Education,* December 3, 1999, pp. A48–A49.

28. James W. Fraser, *Between Church and State: Religion and Public Education in a Multicultural America* (New York: St. Martin's Press, 1999), p. 6.

29. Ibid., p. 133.

30. Marjorie Coeyman, "First-Grader Tests Ban on Religion in Class," *Christian Science Monitor,* June 15, 1999, pp. 1, 5.

31. S. Mark Heim, *Salvations: Truth and Differences in Religion* (Maryknoll, N.Y.: Orbis Press, 1995).

32. See Steven J. Pope, *The Evolution of Altruism and the Ordering of Love* (Washington, D.C.: Georgetown University Press, 1994).

33. Paul Brockelman, *Cosmology and Creation: The Spiritual Significance of Contemporary Cosmology* (New York: Oxford University Press, 1999).

Notes to Chapter One

1. See U. S. News/PBS Religion and Ethics Newsweekly Poll, as reported in "Faith in America: In Troubled Times, How Americans' Views of Religion Are Changing," *U.S. News and World Report,* May 6, 2002, pp. 40–49.

2. See Kenneth I. Pargament, *The Psychology of Religion and Coping: Theory, Research, Practice* (New York: Guilford Press, 1997).

3. Immanuel Jakobovits, *Jewish Medical Ethics* (New York: Block Publishing, 1975), p. 2.

4. For the definitive assessment of more than 1,200 existing studies, see Harold G. Koenig, Michael E. McCullough, and David B. Larson, *Handbook of Religion and Health* (New York: Oxford University Press, 2001).

5. John P. Foglio and Howard Brody, "Religion, Faith and Family Medicine," *Journal of Family Practice* 27 (1988): 473–74.

6. Karl Jaspers, *Psychologie der Weltanschauungen,* 2d ed. (Berlin: Springer, 1931), p. 229; reprinted in *The Worlds of Existentialism,* 2d ed., ed. Maurice S. Friedman (Atlantic Highlands, N.J.: Humanities International, 1991), p. 100.

7. Karl Jaspers, *Philosophy,* trans. E. B. Ashton, revised by Robert G. Leisey (Chicago: University of Chicago Press, 1969–1971), vol. 2, p. 79.

8. Soren Holm, "Jaspers' Philosophy of Religion," in *The Philosophy of Karl Jaspers,* 2d ed., ed. Paul Arthur Schilpp (LaSalle, Ill.: Open Court, 1981), p. 672.

9. Adolph Lichtigfeld, "The Concept of God in Jaspers' Philosophy," in Schilpp, *Philosophy of Karl Jaspers,* p. 700. Some translators have chosen to render Jaspers's term *Grenzsituationen* as "ultimate situations," but the more literal and common translation is "limit situations."

10. Karl Jaspers, in *Karl Jaspers: Basic Philosophical Writings: Selections,* ed. Leonard H. Ehrlich, Edith Ehrlich, and George B. Pepper (Athens: Ohio University Press, 1986), p. 534.

11. Karl Jaspers, *Way to Wisdom,* trans. Ralph Manheim (New Haven, Conn.: Yale University Press, 1954), p. 20. These are lectures Jaspers delivered over Radio Basel in 1949.

12. D. P. Desmond and J. F. Maddux, "Religious Programs and Careers of Chronic Heroin Users," *American Journal of Drug and Alcohol Abuse* 8, no. 1 (1981): 71–83.

13. George E. Valliant, *The Natural History of Alcoholism: Causes, Patterns, and Paths to Recovery* (Cambridge, Mass.: Harvard University Press, 1983).

14. Harold G. Koenig, *The Healing Power of Faith: Science Explores Medicine's Last Frontier* (New York: Simon and Schuster, 1999), p. 86.

15. Ibid., p. 88.

16. David B. Larson, James P. Swyers, and Michael E. McCullough, eds., *Scientific Research on Spirituality and Health: A Consensus Report* (Rockville, Md.: National Institute for Healthcare Research, 1998), pp. 68–82.

17. P. H. Hardesty and K. M. Kirby, "Relation between Family Religiousness and Drug Use within Adolescent Peer Groups," *Journal of Social Behavior and Personality* 10, no. 1 (1995): 421–30; M. L. Adelekan, O. A. Abiodun, A. O. Imoukhomeobayan, G. A. Oni, and O. O. Ogunremi, "Psychosocial Correlates of Alcohol, Tobacco, and Cannabis Use: Findings from a Nigerian University," *Drug and Alcohol Dependence* 33, no. 3 (1993): 247–56; F. Ahmed, D. R. Brown, L. E. Gary, and F. Saadatmand, "Religious Predictors of Cigarette Smoking: Findings from African-American Women of Childbearing Age," *Behavioral Medicine* 20, no. 1 (1994): 34–43.

18. C. D. Emrick, J. Tonigan, H. Montgomery, and L. Little, "Alcoholics Anonymous: What Is Currently Known?" in *Research on Alcoholics Anonymous: Opportunities and Alternatives,* ed. B. S. McCrady

and Willam R. Miller (New Brunswick, N.J.: Rutgers Center of Alcohol Studies, 1993), pp. 41–76; J.M. Williams, J.K. Stout, and L. Erickson, "Comparison of the Importance of Alcoholics Anonymous and Outpatient Counseling to Maintenance of Sobriety among Alcohol Abusers," *Psychological Reports* 58, no. 1 (1986): 803–6; R.L. Gorsuch, "Religious Aspects of Substance Abuse and Recovery," *Journal of Social Issues* 5, no. 12 (1995): 65–83.

19. See various such conversions in William James, *The Varieties of Religious Experience* (1902; reprint, New York: Penguin Books, 1982).

20. Allen E. Bergin, "Religiosity and Mental Health: A Critical Re-Evaluation and Meta-Analysis," *Professional Psychology: Research and Practice* 14 (1983); 170–84; Harold G. Koenig, "Research on Religion and Mental Health in Later Life: A Review and Commentary," *Journal of Geriatric Psychiatry* 23 (1990); 23–53; I.R. Payne, A.E. Bergin, K.A. Bielema, and P.H. Jenkins, "Review of Religion and Mental Health: Prevention and the Enhancement of Psychosocial Functioning," *Prevention in Human Services* 9, no. 2 (1991): 11–40; E.L. Worthington, T.A. Kurusu, M.E. McCullough, and S.J. Sandage, "Empirical Research on Religion and Psychotherapeutic Processes and Outcomes: A 10–Year Review and Research Prospectus," *Psychological Bulletin* 119 (1996): 448–87.

21. E. Idler and S. Kasl, "Religion, Disability, Depression, and the Timing of Death," *American Journal of Sociology* 97, no. 4 (1992): 1052–79; H.G. Koenig, H.J. Cohen, and D.G. Blazer, "Religious Coping and Depression in Elderly Hospitalized Medically Ill Men," *American Journal of Psychiatry* 149 (1992): 1693–1700.

22. K.I. Mation, "The Stress-Buffering Role of Spiritual Support: Cross-Sectional and Prospective Investigation," *Journal for the Scientific Study of Religion* 28, no. 3 (1989): 310–23; S. Wright, C. Pratt, and V. Schmall, "Spiritual Support for Caregivers of Dementia Patients," *Journal of Religion and Health* 24 (1985): 31–38; N. Kruse and T. Van Tran, "Stress Reduction and Religious Involvement among Older Blacks," *Journal of Gerontology, Social Sciences* 44, no. 1 (1989): S4–13.

23. M.Z. Azhar, S.L. Varma, and A.S. Dharap, "Religious Psychotherapy in Anxiety Disorder Patients," *Acta Psychiatrica Scandinavica* 90 (1994): 1–3.

24. C. C. Chu and H. E. Klein, "Psychosocial and Environmental Variables in Outcome of Black Schizophrenics," *Journal of the National Medical Association* 77 (1985): 793–96.

25. H. G. Koenig, L. K. George, and B. L. Peterson, "Religiosity and Remission of Depression in Medically Ill Older Patients," *American Journal of Psychiatry* 155 (1998): 536–42.

26. P. Pressman, J. S. Lyons, D. B. Larson, and J. J. Strain, "Religious Belief, Depression, and Ambulation Status in Elderly Women with Broken Hips," *American Journal of Psychiatry* 147 (1990): 758–59.

27. Pargament, *Psychology of Religion and Coping.*

28. David B. Larson, Francis G. Lu, and James P. Swyers, eds., *Model Curriculum for Psychiatric Residency Training: Religion and Spirituality in Clinical Practice—A Course Outline* (Rockville, Md.: National Institute for Healthcare Research, 1997).

29. Thomas à Kempis, *The Imitation of Christ,* book 1, 12.

30. H. G. Koenig, K. I. Pargament, and J. Nelson, "Religious Coping and Health Status in Medically Ill Hospitalized Older Patients," *Journal of Nervous and Mental Disease* 186 (1998): 513–21.

31. Lynn Underwood-Gordon, "A Working Model of Health: Spirituality and Religiousness as Resources: Applications to Persons with Disability." Unpublished paper, 1995.

32. J. M. Anderson, L. J. Anderson, and G. Felsenthal, "Pastoral Needs for Support within an Inpatient Rehabilitation Unit," *Archives of Physical Medicine and Rehabilitation* 74 (1993): 574–78.

33. W. J. Strawbridge, R. D. Cohen, and S. J. Shema, "Frequent Attendance at Religious Services and Mortality over 28 Years," *American Journal of Public Health* 87 (1997): 957–61.

34. T. E. Oxman, D. H. Freeman, and E. D. Manheimer, "Lack of Social Participation or Religious Strength and Comfort as Risk Factors for Death after Cardiac Surgery in the Elderly," *Psychosomatic Medicine* 57, no. 1 (1995): 5–15.

35. D. Oman and D. Reed, "Religion and Mortality among Community-Dwelling Elderly," *American Journal of Public Health* 88 (1988): 1469–75.

36. Jeffrey S. Levin, "How Religion Influences Morbidity and Health: Reflections on Natural History, Salutogenesis, and Host Resistance," *Social Science and Medicine* 43, no. 5 (1996): 849–64.

37. See review of these studies by Jeffrey S. Levin and Harold Y. Vanderpool, "Is Religion Therapeutically Significant for Hypertension?" *Social Science and Medicine* 29, no. 1 (1989): 69–78.

38. J. W. Dwyer, L. L. Clarke, and M. Miller, "The Effect of Religious Concentration and Affiliation on County Cancer Mortality Rates," *Journal of Health and Social Behavior* 31, no. 2 (1990): 185–202.

39. D. Phillips and E. W. King, "Death Takes a Holiday: Mortality Surrounding Major Social Occasions," *Lancet* 8613 (1995): 728–32.

40. R. W. Williams, D. B. Larson, and R. E. Buckler, "Religion and Psychological Distress in a Community Sample," *Social Science and Medicine* 32 (1991): 1257–62; N. Krause and T. Van Tran, "Stress Reduction"; J. Leserman, E. M. Stuart, M. E. Mamish, and H. Benson, "The Efficacy of the Relaxation Response in Preparing for Cardiac Surgery," *Behavioral Medicine* 15 (1989): 111–17.

41. Levin, "How Religion Influences Morbidity."

42. R. Ader, *Psychoneuroimmunology* (New York: Academic Press, 1981).

43. R. Anda, D. Williamson, and D. Jones, "Depressed Affect, Hopelessness, and the Risk of Ischemic Heart Disease in a Cohort of U. S. Adults," *Epidemiology* 4 (1993): 285–94.

44. J. Kabat-Zinn, L. Lipworth, and R. Burney, "The Clinical Use of Mindfulness Meditation for the Self-Regulation of Chronic Pain," *Journal of Behavioral Medicine* 8 (1985): 163–90.

45. Eric J. Cassel, "The Nature of Suffering and the Goals of Medicine," *New England Journal of Medicine* 306 (1982): 639–45.

46. E. L. Idler and S. V. Kasl, "Religion among Disabled and Nondisabled Persons I: Cross-Sectional Patterns in Health Practices, Social Activities, and Well-Being," *Journal of Gerontology* 52B (1997): S294–305; E. L. Idler and S. V. Kasl, "Religion among Disabled and Nondisabled Persons II: Attendance at Religious Services as a Predictor of the Course of Disability," *Journal of Gerontology* 52B (1997): S306–16.

47. Idler and Kasl, "Religion, Disability, Depression."

48. Oxman et al., "Lack of Social Participation."

49. Dale A. Matthews, Michael E. McCullough, David B. Larson, Harold G. Koenig, James P. Swyers, and Mary Greenwald Milano,

"Religious Commitment and Health Status: A Review of the Research and Implications for Family Medicine," *Archives of Family Medicine* 7 (1998): 118–24.

50. J. K. Kiecolt-Glaser and R. Glaser, "Psychoneuroimmunology and Health Consequences: Data and Shared Mechanisms," *Psychosomatic Medicine* 57 (1995): 267–74.

51. E. M. Sternberg, "Emotions and Disease: From Balance of Humors to Balance of Molecules," *Nature Medicine* 3 (1997): 264–67.

52. Herbert Benson, *Timeless Healing: The Power and Biology of Belief* (New York: Scribner, 1996).

53. Neal Krause, "Neighborhood Deterioration, Religious Coping, and Changes in Health during Late Life," *Gerontologist* 38 (1998): 653–64.

54. See Esther M. Sternberg, ed., *Emotions and Disease* (Bethesda, Md.: National Library of Medicine/National Institutes of Health, 1997).

55. Barbara S. Derrickson, "The Spiritual Work of the Dying: A Framework and Case Studies," *Hospice Journal* 11, no. 2 (1996): 11–30; also J. M. Kaczorowski, "Spiritual Well-Being and Anxiety in Adults Diagnosed with Cancer," *Hospice Journal* 5 (1989): 105–16.

56. Stephen G. Post, "Medicine and Religion," in *The Harper-Collins Dictionary of Religion,* ed. J. Z. Smith and W. S. Green (New York: HarperCollins, 1995), pp. 690–91.

57. F. Scott Peck, *Denial of the Soul: Spiritual and Medical Perspectives on Euthanasia and Mortality* (New York: Harmony Books, 1997).

58. Derrickson, "Spiritual Work of the Dying."

59. W. C. Richard and H. S. Kornfield, *Life to Death: Harmonizing the Transition* (Rochester, Vt.: Inner Traditions, 1995).

60. P. Aries, *Western Attitudes toward Death from the Middle Ages to the Present* (Baltimore, Md.: Johns Hopkins University Press, 1974); Stephen G. Post, *Inquiries in Bioethics* (Washington, D. C.: Georgetown University Press, 1993).

61. C. R. Chapman and J. Gavrin, "Suffering and Its Relationship to Pain," *Journal of Palliative Care* 9 (1993): 5–13.

62. Pargament, *Psychology of Religion and Coping.*

63. B. T. Brandt, "The Relationship between Hopelessness and Selected Variables in Women Receiving Chemotherapy for Breast Cancer," *Oncology Nursing Forum* 14 (1987): 35–39; K. A. Herth, "The

Relationship between Level of Hope and Level of Coping Response and Other Variables in Patients with Cancer," *Oncology Nursing Forum* 16 (1989): 67–72; Eric Kodish and Stephen G. Post, "Oncology and Hope," *Journal of Clinical Oncology* 13 (1996): 1817–22.

64. V. Carson, K. L. Soeken, and P. M. Grimm, "Hope and Its Relationship to Spiritual Well-Being," *Journal of Psychology and Theology* 16 (1988): 159–67.

65. L. A. Gottschalk, J. Fronczek, and M. S. Buchsbaum, "The Cerebral Neurobiology of Hope and Hopelessness," *Psychiatry* 58 (1993): 270–81.

66. M. Z. Azhar and S. L. Varma, "Religious Psychotherapy as Management of Bereavement," *Acta Psychiatrica Scandinavica* 91 (1995): 233–35.

67. M. Galanter, D. B. Larso, and E. Rubenstone, "Christian Psychiatry: The Impact of Evangelical Belief on Clinical Practice," *American Journal of Psychiatry* 148 (1991): 90–95.

68. Oliver Sacks, "The Lost Mariner," in *The Man Who Mistook His Wife for a Hat and Other Clinical Tales* (New York: HarperCollins, 1970), p. 38.

69. Ibid.

70. Ibid.

71. Robert Davis, *My Journey into Alzheimer's Disease: Helpful Insights for Family and Friends* (Wheaton, Ill.: Tyndale House, 1989), p. 55.

72. Ibid., p. 57.

73. Ibid., p. 115.

74. Stephen G. Post, *The Moral Challenge of Alzheimer Disease: Ethical Issues from Diagnosis to Dying,* 2d ed. (Baltimore, Md.: Johns Hopkins University Press, 2000), pp. 84–85.

75. See Hazel Elliot, "Religion, Spirituality and Dementia: Pastoring to Sufferers of Alzheimer's Disease and Other Associated Forms of Dementia," *Disability and Rehabilitation* 19 (1997): 435–41.

76. S. J. Picot, S. M. Debanne, K. H. Namazi, and M. L. Wykle, "Religiosity and Perceived Rewards of Black and White Caregivers," *Gerontologist* 37 (1997): 89–101.

77. Ibid., p. 89.

78. C. Murphey, *Day to Day: Spiritual Help When Someone You Love Has Alzheimer's* (Philadelphia: Westminster Press, 1988).

79. Peter V. Rabins, Melinda D. Fitting, James Eastham, and John Fetting, "The Emotional Impact of Caring for the Chronically Ill," *Psychosomatics* 31 (1990): 334.

80. Ibid.

81. Judy Kaye and Karen M. Robinson, "Spirituality among Caregivers," *Image: Journal of Nursing Scholarship* 26 (1994): 218–21.

82. B. M. Dossey, C. E. Guzzette, and C. V. Kenner, *Critical Care Nursing: Body, Mind, and Spirit* (Philadelphia: J. B. Lippincott, 1991).

83. David B. Larson and Susan S. Larson, *The Forgotten Factors in Physical and Mental Health: What Does the Research Show? An Independent Study Seminar* (Rockville, Md.: National Institute for Healthcare Research, 1994).

84. Larson et al., *Scientific Research on Spirituality and Health.*

85. D. Barnard, R. Dayringer, and C. K. Cassel, "Toward a Person-Centered Medicine: Religious Studies in the Medical Curriculum," *Academic Medicine* 70 (1995): 806–13.

86. D. A. Selway, ed., "Disability, Religion and Health: Exploring the Spiritual Dimensions of Disability," special issue, *Disability and Rehabilitation* 19 (1997).

87. J. S. Levin, D. B. Larson, and C. M. Puchalski, "Religion and Spirituality in Medicine: Research and Education," *Journal of the American Medical Association* 278 (1997): 792–93.

88. Stephen G. Post, "The IRB, Ethics, and the Objective Study of Religion in Health," *IRB: A Review of Human Subjects Research* 17, nos. 5 and 6 (1995): 8–11.

89. William Osler, *A Way of Life: Selected Writings of Sir William Osler* (New York: Dover, 1951), pp. 237–49.

90. D. E. King and B. Bushwick, "Beliefs and Attitudes of Hospital Inpatients about Faith Healing and Prayer," *Journal of Family Practice* 39 (1994): 349–52.

91. T. A. Maugens, "The Spiritual History," *Archives of Family Medicine* 5 (1990): 11–16.

92. T. A. Maugens and W. C. Wadland, "Religion and Family Medicine: A Survey of Physicians and Patients," *Journal of Family Practice* 32 (1991): 210–13.

93. J. A. Roberts, D. Brown, T. Elkins, and D. B. Larson, "Factors Influencing the Views of Patients with Gynecologic Cancer about End-

of-Life Decisions," *American Journal of Obstetrics and Gynecology* 176 (1997): 166–72.

94. K. Schreiber, "Religion in the Physician-Patient Relationship," *Journal of the American Medical Association* 266 (1991): 3062, 3066.

95. M. M. Thiel and M. R. Robinson, "Physicians' Collaboration with Chaplains: Difficulties and Benefits," *Journal of Clinical Ethics* 8, no. 1 (1997): 94–103.

96. T. P. Daaleman and D. E. Nease, "Patient Attitudes Regarding Physician Inquiry into Spiritual and Religious Issues," *Journal of Family Practice* 39 (1994): 564–68.

97. D. B. Larson, A. A. Hohmann, and L. G. Kessler, "The Couch and the Cloth: The Need for Linkage," *Hospital and Community Psychiatry* 39 (1988): 1064–69.

98. Yankelovich Partners, Inc., for TIME/CNN, June 12–13, 1996.

99. A. L. Suchman and D. A. Matthews, "What Makes the Patient-Doctor Relationship Therapeutic?" *Annals of Internal Medicine* 108 (1988): 125–30.

100. *Wall Street Journal,* December 20, 1995, pp. B1, B8.

101. King and Bushwick, "Beliefs and Attitudes of Hospital Inpatients."

102. C. Marwick, "Spiritual Aspects of Well-Being Considered," *Journal of the American Medical Association* 273 (1995): 1561–62.

103. Ninian Smart, *The Study of Religion as a Multidisciplinary and Cross-Cultural Presence among the Human Sciences* (Santa Barbara: University of California, Department of Religious Studies, 1990), p. 7.

104. See Koenig, McCullough, and Larson, *Handbook of Religion and Health.*

105. See G. Ringdal, K. Gotostam, S. Kaasa, S. Kvinnsland, and K. Ringdal, "Prognostic Factors and Survival in a Heterogeneous Sample of Cancer Patients," *British Journal of Cancer* 73 (1995): 1594–99.

Notes to Chapter Two

1. Dalai Lama, *Ethics for the New Millennium* (New York: Riverhead Books, 1999).

2. Augustine, *Confessions,* book 13, 16.

3. Evelyn Underhill, *An Anthology of the Love of God: From the Writings of Evelyn Underhill,* ed. Lumsden Barkway and Lucy Monzies (Wilton, Conn.: Morehouse-Barlow, 1976), p. 30.

4. James H. Austin, *Zen and the Brain: Toward an Understanding of Meditation and Consciousness* (Boston: MIT Press, 1999).

5. Andrew Newberg, Eugene G. d'Aquili, and Vince Rause, *Why God Won't Go Away: Brain Science and the Biology of Belief* (New York: Ballantine Books, 2001).

6. Evelyn Underhill, *The Life of the Spirit and the Life of Today* (1922; reprint, New York: Harper and Row, 1986), p. 5.

7. Ibid., pp. 5–6.

8. Ibid., p. 7.

9. Ibid., p. 10.

10. Ibid., p. 20.

11. A summary of the literature of the neurotheologians can be found in James B. Ashbrook and Carol Rausch Albright, *The Humanizing Brain: Where Religion and Neuroscience Meet* (Cleveland, Ohio: Pilgrim Press, 1997).

12. David B. Larson, James P. Swyers, and Michael E. McCullough, *Scientific Research on Spirituality and Health: A Consensus Report* (Rockville, Md.: National Institute for Healthcare Research, 1997), sec. 5, "Neuroscience," p. 72.

13. Eugene d'Aquili and Andrew B. Newberg, *The Mystical Mind: Probing the Biology of Religious Experience* (Minneapolis, Minn.: Fortress Press, 1999).

14. William James, *The Varieties of Religious Experience* (1902; reprint, New York: Penguin Books, 1982).

15. George Gallup, Jr., *Adventures in Immortality: A Look beyond the Threshold of Death* (New York: McGraw-Hill, 1982).

16. Bruce Greyson, "Biological Aspects of Near-Death Experiences," *Perspectives on Biology and Medicine* 42, no. 1 (1998): 14–32.

17. R. A. Moody, *Coming Back: A Psychiatrist Explores Past-Life Journeys* (New York: Bantam Books, 1991).

18. Greyson, "Biological Aspects," p. 17.

19. Ibid., 24; see myriad articles in the *Journal of Near-Death Studies,* such as E. Rodin, "Comments on 'A Neurobiological Model

for Near-Death Experiences,'" *Journal of Near-Death Studies* 7 (1989): 255–259.

20. Greyson, "Biological Aspects," p. 27.

21. Judith Hooper and Dick Teresi, *The Three-Pound Universe* (New York: Tarcher/Putnam, 1986), p. 330.

22. V. S. Ramachandran, *Phantoms in the Brain: Probing the Mysteries of the Human Mind* (New York: William Morrow, 1998), p. 175.

23. Ibid., p. 183.

24. Ibid., p. 188.

25. Jeffrey L. Saver and John Rabin, "The Neural Substrates of Religious Experience," *Journal of Neuropsychiatry and Clinical Neurosciences* 9 (1997): 498–510.

26. Ibid., p. 507.

27. Ibid.

28. Ibid., p. 508.

29. Joseph LeDoux, *The Emotional Brain: The Mysterious Underpinnings of Emotional Life* (New York: Simon and Schuster, 1996), p. 165.

30. See E. G. d'Aquili and A. B. Newberg, "Religious and Mystical States: A Neuropsychological Model," *Zygon* 28, no. 2 (1993): 177–199.

31. Warren S. Brown, Nancey Murphy, and H. Newton Maloney, eds., *Whatever Happened to the Soul? Scientific and Theological Portraits of Human Nature* (Minneapolis, Minn.: Fortress Press, 1998).

32. Francis Crick, *The Astonishing Hypothesis: The Scientific Search for the Soul* (New York: Charles Scribner's Sons, 1994), pp. 3–4.

33. Ibid., p. 6.

34. Ibid., p. 7.

35. John C. Eccles, *Evolution of the Brain: Creation of the Self* (London: Routledge, 1989), p. 237.

36. Keith Ward, *In Defense of the Soul* (Oxford: Oneworld Publications, 1998); Richard Swinburne, *The Evolution of the Soul* (Oxford: Oxford University Press, 1997).

37. See Nancey Murphy, "Human Nature: Historical, Scientific, and Religious Issues," in Brown et al., *Whatever Happened to the Soul?*, p. 25.

38. Etienne Gilson, *The Spirit of Medieval Philosophy*, trans. A. H. C. Downes (New York: Charles Scribner's Sons, 1936), p. 172.

39. P. E. Meehl and Wilfred Sellars, "The Concept of Emergence," in *Minnesota Studies in the Philosophy of Science*, vol. 1, ed. H. Feigel

and M. Scriven (Minneapolis: University of Minnesota Press, 1956), pp. 239–52.

40. Roy Wood Sellars, *The Philosophy of Physical Realism* (New York: Russell and Russell, 1966).

41. Ibid., p. 87.

42. Malcolm Jeeves, "Brain, Mind and Behavior," in Brown et al., *Whatever Happened to the Soul?* p. 88.

43. Warren S. Brown, "Cognitive Contributions to Soul," in Brown et al., *Whatever Happened to the Soul?* p. 102.

44. For a discussion of emergence, see *Emergence or Reduction? Prospects for Nonreductive Physicalism,* ed. A. Beckermann, H. Flohr, and J. Kim (New York: Walter DeGruyter, 1992).

45. K. S. Kendler, C. O. Gardner, and C. A. Prescott, "Religion, Psychopathology, and Substance Use and Abuse: A Multimeasure, Genetic-Epidemiologic Study," *American Journal of Psychiatry* 154, no. 3 (1997): 322–29.

46. Steven Mithen, *The Prehistory of the Mind: A Search for the Origins of Art, Religion and Science* (London: Phoenix, 1996), p. 172.

47. Ibid., p. 177.

48. Michael Balter, "New Light on the Oldest Art," *Science* 283, no. 12 (February 1999): 920–22.

49. Mithen, *Prehistory of the Mind,* p. 185.

50. Ibid., p. 200.

51. Rudolph Otto, *The Idea of the Holy,* trans. J. H. Harvey (New York: Oxford University Press, 1950).

52. John Baillie, *Our Knowledge of God* (New York: Charles Scribner's Sons, 1930).

53. John Oman, *The Natural and the Supernatural* (New York: Macmillan, 1931).

54. Miercia Eliade, *The Sacred and the Profane,* trans. W. R. Trask (New York: Harcourt, Brace, 1959).

55. Richard J. Degrandpre, "Just Cause? Many Neuroscientists Are All Too Quick to Call a Blip on a Brain Scan the Reason for a Behavior," *Sciences* 39, no. 2 (1999): 15.

56. Gregory Vlastos, "Slavery in Plato's Republic,"*Philosophical Review* 50 (1941): 289–304.

57. David Brion Davis, *The Problem of Slavery in Western Culture* (Ithaca, N.Y.: Cornell University Press, 1966).

58. Wolf Wolfensberger, "The Growing Threat to the Lives of Handicapped People in the Context of Modernistic Values," *Disability and Society* 9, no. 3 (1994): 396.

59. Ibid., p. 400.

60. William E. H. Lecky, *The History of European Morals from Augustus to Charlemagne,* vol. 2 (1869; reprint, New York: George Braziller, 1955), p. 34.

61. Ibid., p. 18.

62. Richard Tarnas, *The Passion of the Western Mind: Understanding the Ideas That Have Shaped Our World View* (New York: Ballantine Books, 1991), p. 116.

63. Nancey Murphy and George Ellis, *The Moral Order of the Universe* (Minneapolis, Minn.: Fortress Press, 1998), p. 217.

64. Ibid.

65. James, *Varieties of Religious Experience,* pp. 272–73.

66. Ibid., p. 274.

67. Ibid., p. 278.

68. Ibid., p. 279.

69. Sir John Templeton, *The Humble Approach: Scientists Discover God* (New York: Continuum, 1995), p. 54.

70. Lee Dugatkin, *Cheating Monkeys and Citizen Bees: The Nature of Cooperation in Animals and Humans* (New York: Free Press, 1998).

71. Matt Ridley, *The Origens of Virtue* (London: Penguin Books, 1996), p. 22.

72. Ibid., p. 84.

73. Ibid., p. 169.

74. Robert Wright, *The Moral Animal* (New York: Pantheon Books, 1994), pp. 12–13.

75. Ibid., p. 368.

76. James Q. Wilson, *The Moral Sense* (New York: Free Press, 1993), p. 192.

77. Ibid., p. 226.

78. Ibid., p. 227.

79. Ibid., p. 43.

80. Ibid., p. 251.

81. Elliot Sober and David Sloan Wilson, *Unto Others: The Evolution and Psychology of Unselfish Behavior* (Cambridge, Mass.: Harvard University Press, 1998), p. 229.

82. See Melvin Konner, *The Tangled Wing: Biological Constraints on the Human Spirit* (New York: Henry Holt, 1982).

83. Peter Singer, *The Expanding Circle: Ethics and Sociobiology* (New York: Meridian Books, 1981), p. 5.

84. Ibid., p. 12.

85. Ibid., p. 20.

86. Ibid.

87. Henri Bergson, *The Two Sources of Morality and Religion*, trans. R. A. Audra and C. Brereton (New York: Doubleday Anchor, 1935), p. 53.

88. Ibid., p. 233.

89. Edward O. Wilson, *On Human Nature* (Cambridge, Mass.: Harvard University Press, 1978), p. 165.

90. Ibid., p. 169.

91. Michael Lerner, *The Politics of Meaning* (Reading, Mass.: Addison-Wesley, 1996), p. 4.

92. Vaclav Havel, *Disturbing the Peace* (New York: Alfred Knopf, 1990), p. 11.

93. Ronald Inglehart, *Culture Shift in Advanced Industrial Society* (Princeton, N.J.: Princeton University Press, 1990), p. 180.

94. "96 Percent Belief in God: Matches 96 Percent Belief Recorded by Gallup 50 Years Earlier, in 1944," *PRRC Emerging Trends*, January 1995, p. 5.

95. See David Myers, "Faith and Society," in *The American Paradox: Spiritual Hunger in an Age of Plenty* (New Haven, Conn.: Yale University Press, 2000), chap. 10.

96. Augustine, *Confessions*, book 10, 22.

97. Thomas, Aquinas, *Summa Theologica*.

98. R. Swinburne, *The Existence of God* (Oxford: Oxford University Press, 1979).

99. Willem B. Drees, *Religion, Science, and Naturalism* (Cambridge: Cambridge University Press, 1996), p. 167.

Notes to Chapter Three

1. Leo Strauss, *Natural Right and History* (Chicago: University of Chicago Press, 1953), p. 127.

2. Jacques Maritain, *Man and the State* (Chicago: University of Chicago Press, 1951), pp. 84–86.

3. Jean Vanier, *Becoming Human* (Mahwah, N.J.: Paulist Press, 1998), p. 22.

4. Melvin Konner, *The Tangled Wing: Biological Constraints on the Human Spirit* (New York: Henry Holt, 1982).

5. Russell Hittinger, *A Critique of the New Natural Law Theory* (Notre Dame, Ind.: University of Notre Dame Press, 1987), pp. 65–92.

6. John Finnis, *Natural Law and Natural Rights* (Oxford: Oxford University Press, 1980), p. 86.

7. Ibid., p. 87.

8. Ibid.

9. Ibid., p. 88.

10. Ibid., p. 89.

11. Ibid., p. 90.

12. Ibid.

13. See Frithjof Bergmann, *On Being Free* (Notre Dame, Ind.: University of Notre Dame Press, 1977).

14. Ibid., p. 380.

15. Anthony J. Lisska, *Aquinas's Theory of Natural Law: An Analytic Reconstruction* (Oxford: Oxford University Press, 1996), pp. 57–64.

16. Alasdair MacIntyre, *Three Rival Versions of Moral Enquiry* (London: Duckworth, 1990), pp. 79–80.

17. Strauss, *Natural Right and History,* p. 129.

18. Heinrich Rommen, *The Natural Law: A Study in Legal and Social History and Philosophy,* trans. T. R. Hanley (London: B. Herder, 1947), p. 86.

19. Ibid., p. 88.

20. Roger J. Sullivan, *Immanuel Kant's Moral Theory* (New York: Cambridge University Press, 1989), pp. 6–7.

21. Reinhold Niebuhr, *The Nature and Destiny of Man,* vol. 1, *Human Nature* (New York: Charles Scribner's Sons, 1941), p. 281.

22. Ibid.

23. Ibid., p. 282.

24. Thomas L. Dumm, *Michel Foucault and the Politics of Freedom* (Thousand Oaks, Calif.: Sage Publications, 1996).

25. See Paul E. Sigmund, ed., *St. Thomas Aquinas on Politics and Ethics* (New York: W. W. Norton, 1988).

26. Niebuhr, *Nature and Destiny of Man,* p. 283.

27. Linda J. Waite and L. A. Lillard, "Til Death Do Us Part: Marital Disruption and Mortality," *American Journal of Sociology* 100 (1995): 1131–56.

28. Judith S. Wallerstein and Joan Berlin Kelley, *Surviving the Breakup* (New York: Basic Books, 1980).

29. Judith S. Wallerstein and Sandra Blakeslee, *Second Chances: Men, Women, and Children a Decade after Divorce* (New York: Ticknor and Fields, 1989).

30. B. L. Bloom, S. W. White, and S. J. Asher, *Divorce and Separation: Context, Causes, and Consequences* (New York: Basic Books, 1979).

31. By far the most thorough compilation of dozens of medical studies is David B. Larson, James P. Swyers, and Susan S. Larson, *The Costly Consequences of Divorce: Assessing the Clinical, Economic, and Public Health Impact of Marital Disruption in the United States* (Bethesda, Md.: National Institute for Healthcare Research, 1995).

32. Andrew J. Cherlin, *Marriage, Divorce, and Remarriage* (Cambridge, Mass.: Harvard University Press, 1992).

33. See Alan Booth and Judy Dunn, eds., *Stepfamilies: Who Benefits? Who Does Not?* (Hillside, N. J.: Lawrence Erlbaum, 1994).

34. Martin Daly and Margo Wilson, "Discriminative Parental Solicitude: A Biological Perspective," *Journal of Marriage and the Family* 42 (1980): 280.

35. Sara McLanahan and Gary Sandefur, *Growing up with a Single Parent* (Cambridge, Mass.: Harvard University Press, 1994), p. 2.

36. Ibid., pp. 30–31.

37. John Courtney Murray, S. J., *We Hold These Truths: Catholic Reflections on the American Proposition* (New York: Sheed and Ward, 1960), pp. 327–28.

38. Leslie Stevenson, *Seven Theories of Human Nature: Christianity, Freud, Lorenz, Marx, Sartre, Skinner, Plato,* 2d ed. (New York: Oxford University Press, 1987), p. 4.

39. Ibid., p. 9.

40. National Secular Society, Office of the Archbishop of Paris, 1991/1998 Comparative Country Data from the International Social Survey Program, 1999.

41. See Carla Power, "Is God Dead? In Western Europe, It Sure Can Look That Way," *Newsweek,* July 12, 1999, pp. 51–55.

42. On secularization and religious decline in western Europe, see José Casanova, *Public Religions in the Modern World* (Chicago: University of Chicago Press, 1994).

43. Stevenson, *Seven Theories,* p. 5.

44. Jean-Paul Sartre, *Nouvel Observateur,* 1980, quoted in Thomas Molnar, "Jean-Paul Sartre," *National Review* 34, no. 11 (1982): 677.

45. See Benedict J. Groeschel, *Stumbling Blocks, Stepping Stones: Spiritual Answers to Psychological Questions* (New York: Paulist Press, 1987), p. 29.

46. Louis Greenspan and Stefan Andersson, *Russell on Religion: Selections from the Writings of Bertrand Russell* (New York: Routledge, 1999).

47. Karen Armstrong, "Where Has God Gone?" *Newsweek,* July 12, 1999, p. 56.

48. Stephen R. L. Clark, *Aristotle's Man: Speculations upon the Aristotelian Anthropology* (Oxford: Clarendon Press, 1974). See Aristotle's *Metaphysics, Book A.*

49. Jacques Maritain, *Man and the State* (1951; reprint, Washington, D.C.: Catholic University Press, 1998), pp. 95–96.

50. Ibid., p. 150.

Notes to Chapter Four

1. Richard J. Rorty, *Achieving Our Country: Leftist Thought in Twentieth-Century America* (Cambridge, Mass.: Harvard University Press, 1997).

2. Richard J. Rorty, "Religion as Conversation-Stopper," chap. 11 in *Philosophy and Social Hope* (New York: Penguin Books, 1999), p. 168.

3. Ibid., p. 169.

4. Ibid.

5. Ibid., p. 170.

6. Ibid., p. 171.

7. Bruce Ackerman, *Social Justice in the Liberal State* (New Haven, Conn.: Yale University Press, 1980).

8. John Rawls, *The Law of Peoples with "The Idea of Public Reason Revisited"* (Cambridge, Mass.: Harvard University Press, 1999), p. 125.

9. Ibid., p. 127.

10. John Rawls, *Political Liberalism* (New York: Columbia University Press, 1993).

11. Ibid., "Introduction," pp. xv–xxxvi, xl.

12. Ibid., p. xxvii.

13. Ibid., p. xxxix.

14. Michael Walzer, *Thick and Thin: Moral Argument at Home and Abroad* (Notre Dame, Ind.: Notre Dame University Press, 1994).

15. In the context of Alasdair MacIntyre's epistemology, "thin" discourse represents the Encyclopedic knowledge of the Enlightenment, which he contrasts with tradition and also defines as a tradition in itself. See Alasdair MacIntyre, *Three Rival Versions of Moral Enquiry: Encyclopedia, Genealogy, and Tradition* (Notre Dame, Ind.: University of Notre Dame Press, 1988).

16. Walzer, *Thick and Thin*, pp. 98–99.

17. Clifford Geertz, *Local Knowledge: Further Essays in Interpretive Anthropology* (New York: Basic Books, 1983).

18. Roy Porter, *The Enlightenment* (New York: Macmillan Press, 1990).

19. Daniel O. Conkle, "Secular Fundamentalism, Religious Fundamentalism, and the Search for Truth in Contemporary America," in *Law and Religion: A Critical Anthology,* ed. Stephen M. Feldman (New York: New York University Press, 2000), p. 321.

20. Michael J. Perry, "Liberal Democracy and Religious Morality," in Feldman, *Law and Religion,* pp. 117–18.

21. Ibid., p. 118.

22. Ibid., p. 119.

23. Richard John Neuhaus, "A New Order of Religious Freedom," in Feldman, *Law and Religion,* p. 89

24. Ibid., p. 90.

25. George M. Marsden, *The Outrageous Idea of Christian Scholarship* (New York: Oxford University Press, 1997), p. 45.

26. See James M. Washington, ed., *I Have a Dream: Writings and Speeches That Changed the World* (San Francisco: Harper, 1992), p. 105.

27. Richard Neuhaus, *The Naked Public Square* (Grand Rapids, Mich.: William B. Eerdmans, 1984), p. 80.

28. Ibid., p. 98.

29. Quoted in ibid.

30. See Martin Luther King, Jr., *Strength to Love* (Philadelphia: Fortress Press, 1963); see also the accounts of the life of King's major mentor, Benjamin Elijah Mays, in Lawrence Edward Carter, Sr., *Walking Integrity: Benjamin Elijah Mays, Mentor to Martin Luther King, Jr.* (Macon, Ga.: Mercer University Press, 1998).

31. Henry P. Van Dusen, *Dag Hammarskjöld: The Statesman and His Faith* (New York: Harper and Row, 1964), p. 3.

32. Ibid., p. 4.

33. Quoted in ibid., p. 150.

34. Telephone survey of 1,015 American adults selected randomly across the United States by the Scripps Howard News Service and the E. W. Scripps School of Journalism of Ohio University, conducted September 22 through October 11, 1999 (margin of error, 4 percentage points).

35. See George Gallup, Jr., and D. Michael Lindsay, *Surveying the Religious Landscape: Trends in U.S. Beliefs* (Boston: Morehouse Publishing, 2000).

36. Ronald F. Thiemann, *Religion in Public Life: A Dilemma for Democracy* (Washington, D.C.: Georgetown University Press, 1996), p. 173.

37. Stephen L. Carter, *The Dissent of the Governed: A Meditation on Law, Religion, and Loyalty* (Cambridge, Mass.: Harvard University Press, 1998).

38. Ibid., p. 28.

39. Kent Greenawalt, *Religious Convictions and Public Choice* (Oxford: Oxford University Press, 1988), p. 113.

40. Ibid., p. 216.

41. Stephen L. Carter, *Civility: Manners, Morals, and the Etiquette of Democracy* (New York: Harper Perennial, 1998).

42. Ibid., p. 18.

43. James Hastings Nichols, *Democracy and the Churches* (Philadelphia: Westminster Press, 1955).

44. Jane Mansbridge, *Beyond Adversarial Democracy* (Chicago: University of Chicago Press, 1983).

45. Stephen G. Post, *More Lasting Unions: Christianity, the Family, and Society* (Grand Rapids, Mich.: William B. Eerdmans, 2000).

46. Joseph Locinte, "Ex-Con: The Remarkable Second Career of Chuck Colson," *Weekly Standard,* June 28, 1999, pp. 21–26.

47. Gilles Kepel, *The Revenge of God: The Resurgence of Islam, Christianity and Judaism in the Modern World,* trans. A. Braley (University Park: Pennsylvania State University Press, 1994).

48. José Casanova, *Public Religions in the Modern World* (Chicago: University of Chicago Press, 1994).

49. Ronald F. Thiemann, *Religion in Public Life: A Dilemma for Democracy* (Washington, D.C.: Georgetown University Press, 1996), p. 73.

50. Ibid., p. 135.

51. Ibid.

52. Ibid., p. 136.

53. Ibid., p. 137.

54. Ibid., p. 139.

55. Ibid., p. 140.

56. Ibid., p. 147.

57. Ibid., p. 148.

58. Ibid., p. 154.

59. Ibid., p. 159.

60. Allen C. Guelzo, *Abraham Lincoln: Redeemer President* (Grand Rapids, Mich.: William B. Eerdmans, 1998).

61. Kathleen Sullivan, "Religion and Liberal Democracy," *University of Chicago Law Review* (1992): 195–223.

62. Michael W. McConnell, "Religious Freedom at the Crossroads," *University of Chicago Law Review* 59 (1992): 115–94.

63. Richard John Neuhaus, "A New Order of Religious Freedom," in Feldman, *Law and Religion,* p. 89.

64. A. James Reichley, *Religion in American Public Life* (Washington, D.C.: Brookings Institute, 1985), p. 117.

65. Stephen V. Monsma, *Positive Neutrality: Letting Religious Freedom Ring* (Ada, Mich.: Baker House, 1995), p. 42.

66. Ibid., p. 51.

67. John Witte, Jr., *Religion and the American Constitutional Experiment: Essential Rights and Liberties* (Boulder, Colo.: Westview Press, 2000), p. 237.

68. Ibid., p. 6.

69. Ibid.

70. Phillip E. Hammond, *With Liberty for All: Freedom of Religion in the United States* (Louisville, Ky.: Westminster John Knox Press, 1998), p. 97.

71. Ibid., p. 106.

72. Ibid.

73. Monsma, *Positive Neutrality,* p. 174.

74. Ibid., p. 176.

75. Ibid., p. 192.

76. Ibid., p. 217.

77. Frederick Mark Gedicks, *The Rhetoric of Church and State: A Critical Analysis of Religion Clause Jurisprudence* (Durham, N.C.: Duke University Press, 1995).

78. James Q. Wilson, *The Moral Sense* (New York: Basic Books, 1995).

79. See Stephen G. Post, *More Lasting Unions: Christianity, the Family, and Society* (Grand Rapids, Mich.: William B. Eerdmans, 2002).

80. T. M. Parker, *Christianity and the State in the Light of History* (London: Adam and Charles Black, 1955), p. 172.

81. Neuhaus, *The Naked Public Square,* p. 82.

82. Ibid., p. 87.

83. Lord Acton, *Essays on Freedom and Power,* ed. Gertrude Himmelfarb (Gloucester, Mass.: Peter Smith, 1972), p. 104.

84. William Temple, *Christianity and the Social Order* (New York: Seabury Press, 1977), p. 72.

Notes to Conclusion

1. See Jacques Maritain, *Man and the State* (Chicago: University of Chicago Press, 1951), p. 86.

2. John T. Noonan, *The Lustre of Our Country: The American Experience of Religious Freedom* (Berkeley: University of California Press, 1998), p. 2.

3. Mark DeWolfe Howe, *The Garden in the Wilderness: Religion and Government in American Constitutional History* (Chicago: University of Chicago Press, 1965), p. 156.

4. Noonan, *The Lustre of Our Country*, p. 1.

5. See Morris R. Cohen, "The Dark Side of Religion," in *The Faith of a Liberal: Selected Essays by Morris R. Cohen* (New York: Henry Holt, 1946), pp. 337–61.

6. Noonan, *The Lustre of Our Country*, p. 1.

7. Ibid., p. 2.

8. Two useful books, after a half century, remain worth noting on the topic of religion and freedom. One is Barbara Ward's *Faith and Freedom* (New York: W. W. Norton, 1954), and the second is James Hastings Nichols, *Democracy and the Churches* (Philadelphia: Westminster Press, 1951).

9. Teilhard de Chardin, *The Phenomenon of Man* (1955; reprint, New York: Harper and Row, 1975), 267.

10. Ibid.

11. Steven Goldberg, *Seduced by Science: How American Religion Has Lost Its Way* (New York: New York University Press, 1999).

12. See, for example, Kitty Ferguson, *Fire in the Equations: Science, Religion, and the Search for God* (Grand Rapids, Mich.: William B. Eerdmans, 1994); Paul Davies, *The Mind of God: The Scientific Basis for a Rational World* (New York: Simon and Schuster, 1993); Errol Harris, *Cosmos and Theos: Ethical and Theological Implications of the Anthropic Cosmological Principles* (Atlantic Highlands, N.J.: Humanities Press, 1992); Robert Jastrow, *God and the Astronomers* (New York: W. W. Norton, 1992); George Johnson, *Fire in the Mind: Science, Faith, and the Search for Order* (New York: Alfred Knopf, 1995); Henry Margenau and Roy A. Varghese, *Cosmos, Bios, Theos: Scientists Reflect on Science, God, and the Origins of the Universe, Life and Homo Sapiens*

(Chicago: Open Court, 1995); Arthur R. Peacocke, *From DNA to Dean: Reflections and Explorations of a Priest-Scientist* (Ridgefield, N.J.: Morehouse Publishing, 1997); John C. Polkinghorne, *The Faith of a Physicist* (Princeton, N.J.: Princeton University Press, 1994); John C. Polkinghorne, *Belief in God in an Age of Science* (New Haven, Conn.: Yale University Press, 1998); Russell Stannard, *Science and Wonders: Conversations about Science and Belief* (London: Faber and Faber, 1996); John Marks Templeton and Robert Herrmann, *Is God the Only Reality? Science Explores the Mystery of the Universe* (New York: Continuum, 1994). Many other works might be cited as well.

13. See Howe, *Garden in the Wilderness.*

14. Jacques Maritain, *Integral Humanism: Temporal and Spiritual Problems of a New Christendom,* trans. Joseph W. Evans (1936; reprint, Notre Dame, Ind.: University of Notre Dame Press, 1968), p. 60.

15. Fergus Kerr, *Immortal Longings: Versions of Transcending Humanity* (Notre Dame, Ind.: University of Notre Dame Press, 1997), p. 169.

Index

STEPHEN G. POST is professor and associate director for educational programs in the department of bioethics at the Case Western Reserve University School of Medicine. He is a senior research scholar at the Becket Institute, St. Hugh's College, Oxford University. Dr. Post has published widely in the area of science and religion. He is the editor-in-chief of the third edition of the five-volume *Encyclopedia of Bioethics,* and was recently named President of the Institute for Research on Unlimited Love-Altruism, Compassion, Service.

Post's perspective privileges no particular religion, but rather asks that adherents to all faiths, including secularism, be allowed freely to express their core values in a civil, respectful, and public manner. Post calls for a recovery of the full meaning of liberal democracy in all domains of public life, so that we might again discover the value of freedom of expression.

STEPHEN G. POST is professor and associate director for educational programs in the department of bioethics at Case Western Reserve University School of Medicine. He is a senior research scholar at the Becket Institute, St. Hugh's College, Oxford University. Dr. Post has published widely in the area of science and religion. He is editor-in-chief of the third edition of the five-volume *Encyclopedia of Bioethics,* and was recently named President of the Institute for Research on Unlimited Love—Altruism, Compassion, Service.